MUST EAT

PARIS

Restaurant
7, rue du Faubourg Montmartre
75009 PARIS 01 47 70 86 29
1896
Charlier
1896

BOUILLON
Charlier
1896   1896

Restaurant
7, rue du Faubourg Montmartre
75009 PARIS 01 47 70 86 29

MUST
EAT
PARIS

AN ECLECTIC SELECTION OF CULINARY LOCATIONS

LUC HOORNAERT
PHOTOGRAPHY: KRIS VLEGELS

LANNOO

Paris…

Paris is a lively city and the global capital of gastronomy. It is a city where the history-rich French kitchen and the young fusion kitchen of the 21st century have reached out to each other. A city where every flavour has its own place, where everything is combined and intertwined, where every chef is enriched by his colleagues, where tradition combines with the sparkle of youth and cultural diversity.

For our taste buds, this means an endless journey. A journey of enjoying the full aroma of dishes in mythical brasseries and bistros, of looking for a table at the many classic or modern star-studded restaurants, and feasting on pho, ceviche or a different type of dimsum, only to continue our journey further through the streets of the city of lights searching for thousands of other dishes and experiences.

The English poet, William Cowper wrote: "Variety's the very spice of life that gives it all its flavour." I absolutely agree with this and I think that this profuse selection is precisely what makes Paris so charming. So much variety stimulates creativity and cross-pollination and opens a dialogue among people. After all, the kitchen is the story of people and products.

Sitting at the table, people converse, flirt, sometimes argue, enjoy and wander off, but always together. And what could be nicer and more essential than sharing a moment, a smile, a dish?

Chef David Toutain

CONTENTS

le salon 👈

la cuisine 👈

CLAUS

14 Rue Jean-Jacques Rousseau - 75001 Paris
T +33 1 42 33 55 10
Mon.-Fri. 07.30-18.00; Sat.-Sun. 09.30-17.00

After a breath-taking evening with your significant other in the city of love and romance,
you might want to follow this up with a delicious and romantic breakfast.

Rösti, smoked salmon, sour cream with dill, pouched egg with a little salad

Everything here is homemade, except for the bread that every morning is picked up freshly baked from a likeminded baker.

For a city so obsessed with good food, breakfast in Paris can too often leave you hungry. Poor coffee, over-baked croissants and baguettes are a downright disgrace for a city like Paris. The French don't really consider breakfast to be a meal. Lunch and dinner – these are the real meals. In this abundance of local cafés and hotels with industrial breakfasts, Claus is a welcoming oasis. Claus Estermann, the founder and owner of Claus, is totally dedicated to the most important meal of the day. He believes that breakfast is a meal in itself. Breakfast must be sweet and hearty, warm and cold, but in former days, this was totally unheard of in Paris.

This charming tea-room is located literally amidst luxury boutiques and offices. You can have a lavish breakfast at the location in a very cosy salon or you can take away your favourite breakfast. One thing is certain: everything that you eat here is absolutely top quality. Moreover, to meet the demand for qualitative take-out breakfasts, Claus has opened a boutique across the street from his salon where you can find everything you need for a royal breakfast.

Claus Estermann, who originates from Bavaria, decided to share his love for a hearty breakfast with the citizens of his adopted city. Therefore, he decided to open this very cosy breakfast salon in the vicinity of Les Halles. Here the atmosphere is key. On the first floor is a kitschy little salon with whitewood tables in contrast to the pine green colour of the floor.

Everything here is homemade, except for the bread that every morning is picked up freshly baked from a like-minded baker. Everything is meticulously selected; the eggs come from a trusted farm outside of the city. In the early years of the restaurant, his greatest pleasure was personally to pick up the bread early in the morning from the baker. Cycling at dawn over the Pont Neuf, totally alone, with his legs warmed up from the hot bread in his bike bags, made him intensely happy.

At Claus, breakfast is a form of art.

KEI

5 Rue Coq Héron - 75001 Paris
T +33 1 42 33 14 74 - www.restaurant-kei.fr
Tue.-Sat. 12.30-14.00 and 19.30-21.00

I really have the impression that super-talented Japanese chefs are gradually taking over the Parisian culinary scene. At the helm of this top restaurant is the extremely talented Keisuke Kobayashi.

Creations of nature

At a young age, Kei had a revelation: After watching a culinary programme with his mouth wide open, the young fellow decided that he would become a chef when he grew up. When he was a bit older, he was totally blown away by a meal at an excellent restaurant in Nagano, where they served French food exclusively. He embarked on a serious research journey through the French countryside in order to get a better understanding of the depth and richness of French gastronomy.

He worked at Auberge du Vieux Puits in Fonjoncuse, Le Prieuré in Ville-neuve-lès-Avignon and Le Cerf in Mer-lenheim, to name a few – all of which are highly regarded and starred restaurants. When, in 2003, he was allowed to join the team of Alain Ducasse and work under Jean-François Piège in the kitchens of Plaza Athénée, his talent exploded. By 2011, the time was ripe to start his own place, and he opened Kei.

This story fits in with the new wave: Japanese chefs are increasingly becoming masters of the art of French cooking and even excel in it. Their restaurants are usually very unobtrusive and the names are difficult to find. The Japanese tradition of *omakase* – whereby, unlike á la carte, the chef selects what to serve the guests depending on the quality of his ingredients – is fully respected. Their food is naturally precise, focused and always season-based, which for a Japanese top chef is self-evident whether he is cooking in Japan or in France. Their presentations are usually breathtakingly beautiful. Currently, there are around 500 Japanese chefs in Paris alone. Of course, they are not all top chefs, but they are all in demand due to their great devotion.

There was a time when Japanese chefs came to be trained in the great French culinary temples, because it looked good on their CVs. Nowadays, they stay in France and challenge their teachers.

Kei serves food that could just as well have come from Japan, but with great French ingredients. He combines what appears to be effortless aesthetics, harmony, poetry and the natural with a typical balance between texture and taste. Two worlds meet in this restaurant and Kei considers himself neither a Japanese chef nor a French chef; he is simply the Kei chef. The result is total subtlety, fragility and balance in its purest form.

Kei is a truly great chef with immense talent as pure as crystal.

Cochon

LOUP

- Petits déjeuners
- Organic eggs
- English breakfast
- Plat du jour
- Tasse-croûtes
  des Halles

Menu "Petits loups"
12€

Drink & Food
any time

LOVE FOOD

L'APPÉTIT SAUVAGE

LOUP

LOUP

44 Rue du Louvre - 75001 Paris
T +33 1 42 36 73 23 - www.-paris.fr
Daily 08.00-24.00

Gosh, what a nice place! Loup meets the modern demands of new restaurant goers.
But is it really a restaurant?

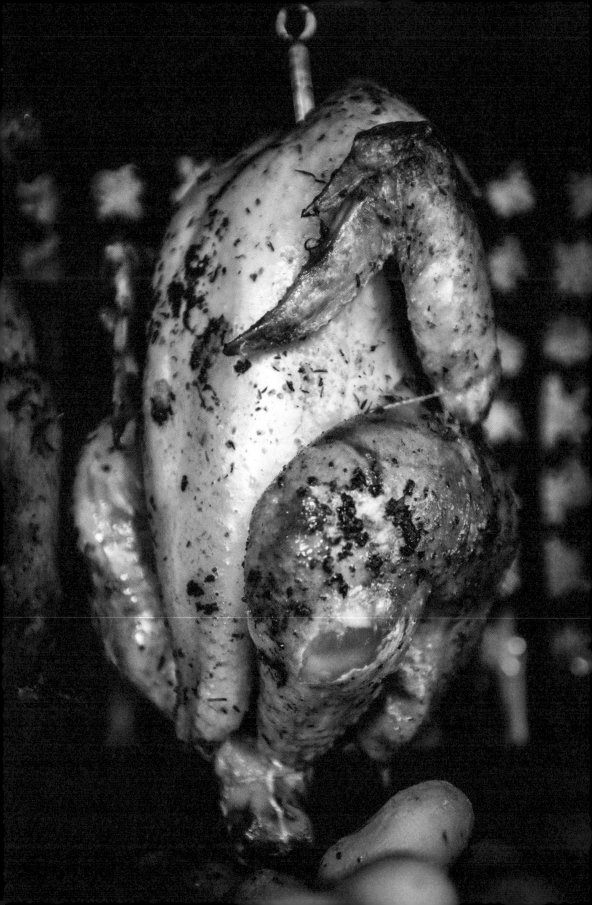

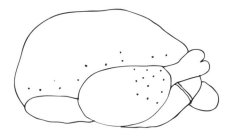

Père Godard free-range chicken

Is there any dish that better qualifies as comfort food?

Not really, it's more than that. It's a place you go to when you want to chat, to nibble, to eat, to have breakfast, brunch, etc. The interior design is based on the history of the neighbourhood; after all we are talking about Les Halles. It is mainly a very attractive spot that will definitely not leave you indifferent. The general theme is rather pastoral. The hall is dominated by a monumental elk head, which seems to have been shot by one of the Godards; this mighty animal weighed 1.2 tonnes.

What attracted me with irresistible force is the rotisserie where several oversized fatted chickens (poulards) are turning at the top and a generous piece of delicious looking pork is slowly roasting at the bottom. The free-range chicken of *Père Godard* is famous due to its wonderful quality. Étienne Godard is a third-generation poultry farmer in the Périgord region and specialises in uncompromising quality of various fowl. And his range of fowl is unique! Just the sight of those lovely whole chickens brings on my hunger pangs. Just the idea of the crispy chicken skin on my plate with a juicy and tasty drumstick is too overwhelming. Is there any dish that better qualifies as comfort food than a perfectly roasted chicken? Chef Teyant certainly makes it his duty to honour his old-fashion rotisserie.

I would really like to spend an entire day here in order to observe everyone, from the early breakfasters to the night birds. Get totally absorbed in the wonderful mix that you find here. Businessmen, fashion models, weirdos from the neighbourhood, artists, hipsters, creative people... Everyone finds something here to his liking and feels good at.

PIROUETTE

5 Rue Mondétour - 75001 Paris
T +33 1 40 26 47 81
Mon.-Sat. 12.00-16.00 and 19.00-24.00

In the pedestrian part of les Halles there are lots of restaurants,
but I am convinced that Pirouette has no competition in this neighbourhood.

Breaded white asparagus

The Pirouette adventure began in 2012 when Laurent and Jean-Marie Fréchet combined forces and decided to open a nice restaurant with everything that goes with it.

Pirouette is a beautiful brasserie in the classic sense of the word and it's spacious with a great deal of natural light penetrating through the windows. The freedom to choose is imperative. No menus, fixed prices or other formulas, but straight à la carte, as it should be in any self-respecting brasserie.

The man who proved this is Tomy Gousset, who worked long enough in the kitchens of Le Meurice and Daniel

Boulud (New York City) to develop his own contemporary view of brasserie food.

Pirouette creates perplexing dilemmas, such as choosing one dish from the menu when you want to try everything. Therefore, this is the type of restaurant where you should eat with a 'switch partner'. You know what I mean – someone with whom you can unabashedly switch dishes in the middle of every course, so that you can taste a lot more dishes.

The beautiful interior, the brilliant wine list and the amazing food are together far greater than what you would expect at these prices.

YAM'TCHA

121 Rue St-Honoré - 75001 Paris
T +33 1 40 26 08 07 - www.yamtcha.com
Tue. 20.00-21.30; Wed.-Sat. 12.00-14.00 and 20.00-21.30

Yam tcha in Cantonese literally means 'drinking tea', but it is also the term for drinking tea in the morning with the family and that usually means eating a few *dim sums*.

Horse mackerel in white wine, coulis of goose liver and spinach

Additionally, it is the Cantonese word for *dim sum.* Yam'Tcha exposes the essence of this restaurant: tea. Tea plays an important role in the life of Adeline Grattard and her husband Chi Wah Chan who is a tea sommelier and runs a small and exclusive tea boutique in the city. But wine lovers need not fear, Adeline from Burgundy does not deny her origins. Wine here is just as important – and not only wine from Burgundy.

The couple opened this small and hidden gem in 2009 just after they returned from Hong Kong. It became an exquisite fusion restaurant, very intimate and quiet. For the maximum twenty people that could originally fit into the restaurant, it was a real journey to the heart of China (and too bad – also back).

Grattard is the boss in her 4-square metre kitchen from where she manages the restaurant. Her kitchen is surprising and offers an insight into how a genuine fusion chef thinks and works. In general, the fusion kitchens in France infuse French dishes with Asian tones. Thanks to her two-year apprenticeship under the guidance of various chefs in Hong Kong, Grattard has a totally different perspective on this and was able to really master the kitchens of southern China. No run-of-the-mill fusion dishes, but *the real McCoy.* Daily changing creations according to what Adeline finds and prepares that day.

After moving, the restaurant has doubled in floor space and also enjoys more daylight that provides a very special atmosphere. The interior décor combines a bit of Paris chic and oriental fantasy in which the paper lanterns, frescos and Carrara marble also play a role.

The tough learning period at Pascal Barbot (L'Astrance) followed by two years in Hong Kong have been quite lucrative for Adeline. She has the focus and concentration of a Shaolin monk and her dishes reflect inner peace.

Yam'Tcha is hot! This restaurant is not only about phenomenal food and haute cuisine with a lot of Chinese influence, it is also a place to cherish, a place where you are received differently and where generosity is of paramount importance.

ADDITIONAL EATERIES
LES HALLES /
CENTRE POMPIDOU /
LOUVRE

ELLSWORTH
34 Rue de Richelieu, 75001 Paris
T +33 1 42 60 59 66
www.ellsworthparis.com
Mon. 19.00-22.30; Thu.-Sat. 12.30-14.30 and 19.00-22.30;
Sun. 11.30-15.00

FISH CLUB
58 Rue Jean-Jacques Rousseau, 75001 Paris
T +33 1 40 26 68 75
Thu.-Sat. 20.00-23.00

LE 404
Rue des Gravilliers, 75003 Paris
T +33 1 42 74 57 81
www.404-resto.com
Sun.-Thu. 12.00-15.00 and 19.30-01.00;
Fri.-Sat. 12.00-15.00 and 19.30-02.00

SATURNE
17 Rue Notre Dame des Victoires, 75002 Paris
T +33 1 42 60 31 90
www.saturne-paris.fr
Mon.-Fri. 12.00-14.30 and 20.00-22.30

KASPIA

17 Place de la Madeleine - 75008 Paris
T +33 1 42 65 33 32 - www.caviarkaspia.com
Mon.-Sat. 12.00-01.00

Whenever you sit in the monumental Place de la Madeleine to eat caviar in this historical establishment, you really feel the decadence of Paris. You are sitting in one of the most beautiful cities in the world, at one of the most charming plazas and are eating the most divine delicacy. Things can't get any better!

Caviar à go-go

Back in 1927, Arcady Fixon opened a caviar trade attached to a restaurant. Its success convinced him in 1953 to move the business to its current location on Place de la Madeleine. In this restaurant, you can endlessly admire the antique artefacts, a collection that belongs to the founder. The atmosphere is definitely pre-revolutionary. It seems as if several times a day the waiters re-enact the scene from Anna Karenina where Oblonsky orders a bottle of champagne. Did Tolstoy already have Kaspia in mind in 1875?

Kaspia is chic, classic chic. Yet, it seems that this old-fashioned elegance attracts a very modern clientele. You will find an eclectic mix of guests, politicians, gallery owners, Jay-Z & Beyoncé, philosophers, intellectuals and a multitude of modern style icons. The best of Paris high society frequents this restaurant that looks more like a private club. The insiders call it the caviar cafeteria and even on quiet evenings a conspiratorial atmosphere reigns as these insiders all consider themselves to be just at the right place. The restaurant is located on the second floor and you have to go through the store to reach it. From the street, you don't realise that there is a restaurant up there. It looks like a real secret society; the only thing missing is a secret handshake of the members.

Caviar is naturally the highlight in this luxurious top restaurant without frills. A nice menu might include seven different caviar preparations, some goose liver, smoked fish and a nice salad.

The most popular dish here is crab salad followed by the *pomme muscovite* (muscovite potato), naturally served with a mother-of-pearl spoon. In addition, it can be topped with the best Beluga or with salmon eggs, but then you must order a Vladivostock.

There is only one Kaviar Kaspia and in a world where it is normal to blur moral standards, this spot is truly a respite and a place of refuge. Luxury still exists and the modern Oblonskys will find it delightful. You don't need a special occasion to dine here; just being here is a special occasion.

NODAIWA

272 Rue Saint-Honoré - 75001 Paris
T +33 1 42 86 03 42 - www.nodaiwa.com
Mon.-Sat. 12.00-14.30 and 19.00-22.00

Very few people can surmise the kind of subtle flavours that are concealed behind this discreet façade. Once you open the door, a very specific, delicious and subtle scent takes you directly to a typical *unagi* (eel) restaurant in Japan.

Unagi no Kabayaki

Caramelised eel

This scent that comes from a slow smouldering *binchotan,* using white charcoal, which in addition to providing a source of heat, also provides seasoning for the subtle taste. During the Genroku period (1688-1704) this top-quality charcoal was first produced by Bitchu-ya Chozaemon in Tanabe, Wakayama Prefecture. He used only very old ubame oak. The very special character of this very high quality charcoal – favoured by robata, yakitori and unagi cooks – is achieved by steaming the oak at very high temperatures.

This establishment makes the famous caramelised eel. I am personally convinced that every culinary entity has its own speciality and I am of the opinion that nowhere in the world is there a better eel recipe than the one prepared at the Japanese unagi no kabayaki. A wonderful preparation in which the eel is carefully opened, not pillaged. Subsequently, the filet is grilled and steamed as a single piece and then caramelised on the grill into a heavenly delicacy. This recipe has been inscribed in the *Manyoshu,* a collection of Japanese poems and stories written between 313 and 759 BC which contain various instructions for achieving the gustative qualities of Gamayaki – as eel was then called – by grilling it on an open fire. Somewhat later, during the Edo period,

a certain Noda Iwajiro created the basis for the Kabayaki recipe. He established Nodaiwa, a restaurant that flourished during the Edo period and which attracted people from far and wide. The secret was in the complex sauce made from eel bones, soya, saké, mirin (mild saké) and a few other secret ingredients. Since that period, a distinction is made between the Kanto (Tokyo) and the Kansai (Osaka) methods of filleting eels. In Kanto, they are filleted along the back, in Kansai along the belly. This tradition dates back to Samurai warrior culture, when opening the eel through the belly symbolised hara-kiri – a form of Japanese ritual suicide that involved cutting open the abdomen with a sword.

A traditional restaurant such as Nodaiwa obviously offers far more than just grilled eel. It also serves Nikogori, a piece of eel in an eel jelly as a type of eel desert, or Nanbanzuke, marinated and fried pieces of eel. Arai is lightly poached eel with pieces of yuzu and the Kimoyaki, grilled eel liver, is a real delicacy. Matsukaze is a type of eel pie with sesame and Tsukadani is eel cooked with ginger. Complete your meal with eel sushi and you'll have the best day ever.

ADDITIONAL EATERIES

MADELEINE /
OPÉRA /
PLACE DES VOSGES

BIEN BIEN
30 Rue Bergère
75009 Paris
T +33 1 48 24 14 42

BIZAN
56 Rue Sainte-Anne
75002 Paris
T +33 1 42 96 67 76
Thu.-Sat. 12.00-14.00 and 19.30-22.00

ATELIER RODIER

17 Rue Rodier - 75009 Paris
T +33 1 53 20 94 90 - www.latelier-rodier.com
Thu.-Sat. for lunch, reservation is mandatory, dinner from 19.00 onwards

Santiago Torrijos was born in Columbia and discovered France when he was eighteen.
At that period of his life he was completely focused on architecture.

Braised beef, purée, spinach, celeriac, parsnip, blood orange gel, kumquat, spicy beef gravy

A classic!

A career in cooking never entered his mind even though his uncle was a chef in Columbia and always told him that being a travelling chef was the best way to discover new cities and cultures. He trained in a restaurant in St-Germain. Meanwhile he lived in Paris, where his mother was also living.

Later and full of motivation, he studied for five years at the famous École Drouant in Paris. His first real training was at Fouquet under the helm of Alexandre Faix, who was then the youngest starred chef in France. He has taught Santiago everything that he now knows and does.

After this training period, he went to work at Robuchon, which was still located on Rue Poincarré. He first worked in the dining room, but soon discovered that his real passion was in the kitchen. Precision, strictness, military discipline and sleeplessness are the words he remembers from that period. His career was soon shaped by Le Grand Véfour, where Guy Martin took him under his wing. That was followed by Veyrat, and later he worked at Le Bristol Paris with head chef, Eric Fréchon.

After a sabbatical, during which he travelled a great deal, he came back and landed up with Christophe Moret, chef of Plaza Athénée.

Three years ago, while walking past premises on Rue Rodier in the 9th arrondissement, he decided to follow his dream. After making sweeping changes to the physical location, Atelier Rodier was ready. It looks reasonably simple, but has a substantial look nevertheless. His dishes had a simple and classic structure, but demonstrated a great deal of experience and craftsmanship.

Columbian dishes were not originally part of his menu, but after the first few months, Santiago gained more self-confidence and decided to put some items from Bogota – his home turf – on the menu, but according to his own interpretation. That way he elevated Changua, a poor man's dish, into a culinary tour de force. This meal, usually eaten in Columbia on Sundays, is a rich milk soup that includes bread, poached eggs, coriander and spring onions. His own version has become one of his classics, just like the Carne a la Llanera.

Atelier Rodier is a hidden gem in Paris.

AUTOUR DU YANGTSE

12 Rue du Helder - 75009 Paris
T +33 1 53 34 05 78
Mon.-Sat. 12.00-15.00 and 18.30-22.30

Dim, ergo sum.
Dim sum is no doubt my favourite way of eating.

Xia Long Bao

a real delicacy, a play of textures for your taste buds

I'm always immensely impressed by the speed with which real dim sum restaurants can conjure an unbelievable variety of tastes and forms. Everyone enjoys the dishes and it is super-cosy.

Contrary to popular belief, dim sum is not a specific snack; it refers to a way of eating. It literally means 'touch the heart'. In Cantonese, people talk about *yum cha,* which means 'drinking tea'. This better reveals the roots of dim sum. It originates from the Silk Route period, when rest stops were set up for the many travellers and tea and small snacks were served. Many of the most daring meals were dim sum meals.

One of the most craved for dim sum was no doubt the *xia long bao,* which originates in Shanghai and Wuxi. They are traditionally prepared in xia long, the typical bamboo baskets that nowadays are inextricably linked to dim sum. The xia long bao originated in Nanxiang, a suburb of Shanghai in the Jiading district. The inventor, Huang Mingxian, had a modest food stall near Guyi Garden, the most prominent park in Shanghai. He wanted to make something creative in order to attract more customers and conceived of a way to get soup in a dim sum. This was around 1880 and henceforth this delicacy began to spread very fast. There are still two traditional xia long bao restaurants in the original neighbourhood. Nanxiang Mantou Dian is the continuation of the original spot where the inventor's stall stood and it is located in the Yu Garden. Here the dim sum is made mainly with crab. In the other restaurant, Gulong, dim sum is traditionally prepared with meat.

Behind the walls of this modest eatery, you will find the only place in Paris that prepares this unique dim sum. A xia long bao is a real delicacy, a play of textures for your taste buds. You get a consommé that's so tasty you will think your mouth is bursting; the wonderful bite of meat or crab filling and then the silky feel of the dough sheet – all that fragilely held together. A perfect bite that gradually releases its tastes in your mouth.

BOUILLON CHARTIER

7 Rue du Faubourg Montmartre - 75009 Paris
T +33 1 47 70 86 29 - www.bouillon-chartier.com
Daily 11.30-00.00

Bouillon Chartier is a perfectly preserved relic of Parisian history. It is a *bouillon,* which is a very large and traditional restaurant where people can eat quickly at affordable prices. Most of these restaurants used to serve mainly bouillon soups, which is where the name comes from.

Pot-au-feu

French beef stew

The first *bouillons* appeared in Paris in 1855 because a shrewd butcher, Pierre-Louis Duval, had the brilliant idea of feeding a sort of pot-au-feu (French beef stew) to people who worked in Les Halles. By 1900, there were already around 250 such restaurants in the city. Actually, they were the first successful theme restaurant and their reputation spread like wild fire throughout the city. Some were even a little high-class and also provided a reading corner or entertainment.

In the meantime, art nouveau spread through Europe. The World's Fairs that took place in Paris in 1878, 1889 and 1900 accelerated the popularity of the *bouillons* in terms of architecture, furnishing and décor and some bouillons were set up in complete art nouveau style.

In 1896, the brothers, Frédéric and Camille Chartier opened the Bouillon Chartier. They chose an abandoned railway station hall. As a result of its immense success, they opened additional Chartiers: one together with Louis Trezel and two other locations on Rue Racine and Boulevard de Montparnasse. The one on Rue Racine reflects a very Baroque and expressive style of Art Nouveau.

Bouillon Chartier is still very much alive and kicking; it doesn't take reservations and everyday hungry people queue up to get inside, though once they reach the revolving doors it goes quite quickly. The experience here is truly like eating in the Paris of yesterday, where nothing has changed. The bill is scribbled on the disposable tablecloth and you'll often find yourself sharing a table with other guests. All this contributes to the immensely positive vibe and atmosphere of this place.

Since its opening, Bouillon Chartier has served approximately 50 million meals. Denon Anselme, the chef who steers everything in the right direction, is a hard-working fellow with a pleasant disposition. His kitchen runs at full speed and everything is freshly prepared. Most of the stringently selected suppliers have been working with them for years and have built a strong bond of trust.

Everyone has eaten here: big names on romantic but anonymous dates, dignitaries and many more who have contributed to the personality and soul of this place. Just look around and enjoy the motion, the dynamics of such a unique place – you are right in the thick of it!

The day that Chartier closes its doors will be a black day for Paris, because there is only one Chartier.

BRASSERIE FLO

7 Cour des Petites Ecuries - 75010 Paris
T +33 1 47 70 13 59 - www.groupeflo.com/brasseries-flo
Sun.-Thu. 12.00-15.00 and 19.00-23.00; Fri.-Sat. 12.00-15.00 and 19.00-24.00

When I visited Paris with my parents at the age of 12, I was impressed by the Eiffel Tower and the many other monuments. As a young adolescent, I discovered the city in my own way to the tunes of *J'aime Paris au mois de mai* of Charles Aznavour.

Traditional, French brasserie cuisine

To go out dining, a taxi brought us to a dark alley in what looked to a 12-year-old like a rough neighbourhood. The taxi driver mumbled some instructions and we disappeared into the darkness. The location where we found ourselves was completely chaotic, or it looked that way at any rate.

It was just before nine, and we squeezed our way through the crowd outside to the reception desk where my father proudly announced: "I have a reservation for nine o'clock." Our name was duly noted and we were told to wait in line along with the rest of the crowd. The idea of getting anything to eat that evening began to evaporate and was replaced by images of gloomy, stale chunks of baguette. At a quarter past nine, a man came outside and attempted to call our typical Flemish name in French. At least ten people desperately raised a finger in the air.

Just as a very hungry me was about to negotiate with the *maître écailler* who guarded his seafood zealously, we were led inside. I felt like a male Alice in Wonderland. Neatly dressed waiters, shining copper, incredible buzzing of pleasant voices and a tower of shellfish. The shellfish specialist had really gone to town.

In 1901, a certain Mr. Floberger purchased the charming premises which he converted it into a cosy Alsatian beer hall. The approaching war forced him to shorten the name from Floberger to Flo. In this neighbourhood, close to the Gare du Nord and the Gare de l'Est, barrels of beer from Alsace have been imported since 1871. Thus, cosy pubs were the order of the day in those times. While in another part of Paris, students were carrying out a revolution, Jean-Paul Bucher, an Alsatian, took over Flo, literally one hour before Charles De Gaulle announced on the radio that the parliament had been dissolved.

Today, more than 4000 people worldwide work for Bucher and Flo has developed into a concept. For me, Flo is the mother of all brasseries and one of the most impressive monuments of Paris.

COMME CHEZ MAMAN

5 Rue des Moines - 75017 Paris
T +33 1 42 28 89 53 - www.commechezmaman.com
Daily 12.00-14.30, Sun.-Wed. 19.00-22.30, Thu.-Sat. 19.00-23.00

I am deeply and unconditionally amazed by Wim Van Gorp. He is one of the best Belgian chefs and he quickly realised that his vision on cooking, eating and dishes would be too innovative for a small country like Belgium.

Wim's inspiration

At one of the most illustrious cookery schools in Europe, located in Koksijde, student chefs came to observe, taste and admire Wim's work. He is one of the top chefs of his generation and this does not escape the minds of the greatest international chefs. That's how Wim caught the attention of Alain Ducasse and Jean-Georges Vongerichten. For the latter, he totally set up a Parisian outpost, The Market. Yet Wim's guts and talent did not go unnoticed by someone such as Vongerichten. Initially, Wim perfectly complemented Vongerichten's particular style, and the two quickly interacted until Wim's successful dishes found their way to various restaurants in NYC via the circuit of Vongerichten.

But after eight years, Wim exchanged the trendy 8th arrondissement of Paris for his own spot in the more popular and authentic Batignolles district in the 17th arrondissement. The Rue des Moines is a lovely street with many top butchery, poultry, fish and vegetable stores that display and market a wealth of wonderful French products. Here, near the covered market of Batignolles, where pastis don't cost you an arm and a leg, super chef Wim has opened a lovely modest restaurant, Comme Chez Maman, where food is prepared in the way that our mothers used to cook.

Wim's masterly hand provides this place with a contemporary view of daily cooking, the home kitchen, and he does that with his typical talent and devotion. The nice result of selecting this neighbourhood is that here you can always find a wonderful mix of locals and incidental eaters. A blackboard is the only place where you can peruse the daily menu. It is neither Wim's style nor his ambition to be confined by a fixed menu. Moreover, Wim shows that he is at home in all the markets. It makes no difference whether a dish is Asian-inspired or made according to a classic repertoire; balance is the key word.

The restaurant is homey and cosy; the dishes are international and modern, yet they always offer enough to cherish because of their traditional roots.

This down-to-earth son of the Kempen just has it in him, the touch of a genius that separates him from the rest. Three stars are definitely within his reach; he hasn't acquired them simply because he has decided not to.

Super!

LE COQ RICO

98 Rue Lepic - 75018 Paris
T +33 1 42 59 82 89 - www.lecoqrico.com
Daily 12.00-14.30 and 19.00-23.00

I could spend hours staring hypnotised at the rotisserie slowly turning various types of fowl until they become gold-brown delicacies.

Grilled Challans chicken

This simple bistro rotisserie belongs to Antoine Westermann, the man brought us amazing restaurants such as Drouant and Mon Vieil Ami. This revamped version of a simple rotisserie gives the feel of a luxury chalet in St-Anton, yet the highest mountain in this neighbourhood is the Hill of Montmartre.

A rotisserie specialising in chicken and eggs; why didn't I come up with this brilliant idea? Practically everything here spins around the chicken and the egg.

Often, the simplest dishes are the most difficult to continuously duplicate and serve at a constant high level. Grilled chicken with French fries and salad is simply the benchmark, a standard that one should store alongside the platinum rule used as the benchmark of one metre at the International Bureau of Weights & Measures. Yup, an officially registered standard for chicken with French fries and salad! Chef Thierry Lébé apparently knows how to work magic with chicken and other types of fowl as he mans the rotisserie spit like a captain steering his ship.

To me, his fowl are like a parade on a turning catwalk. For just a second I think of the other side of the street where the legendary Moulin de la Galette is located and where in earlier years Parisian beauties danced the Cancan. Pintade fermière d'Auvergne (Auvergne farm-reared guinea-fowl), poulet patte noire de Challans (Challans black chicken leg), poulet fermier du Maine (Maine farm-reared chicken), poulet de Bresse (Bresse chicken), pigeon du Poitou (Poitou pigeon)... you name it. These are difficult moments for people who want to taste and try everything; after all, which honourable foodie doesn't dream of comparing a *Poulet de Bresse* with a *Poulet de Challans?*

To keep the evening chicken-only, there are also masterly egg dishes and the inevitable dish with the less noble parts of the chicken – stomach, heart, liver...

In all aspects, a lovely restaurant with a high standard and serious ambition. It's chicken tonight.

GARE AU GORILLE

68 Rue des Dames - 75017 Paris
T +33 1 42 94 24 02
Mon.-Fri. 12.15-14.00 and 19.30-22.00

Georges Brassens, the renowned French singer and poet, has composed soul-stirring music on his guitar to more than one hundred of his poems as well as to texts of Victor Hugo, Paul Verlaine and Luis Aragon.

GEORGES
BRASSENS
la mauvaise réputation et ses belles chansons

GARE AU GORILLE

69

MONTMARTRE / GRANDS BOULEVARDS / PLACE DE CLICHY / PIGALLE

Inspiration of the day

In his first album *La Mauvaise Réputation,* there is a remarkable song called *Le Gorille,* which is full of hidden anarchistic messages and double meanings.

Louis Langevin, the owner and the soul of this restaurant, is an absolute fan of Brassens and named his restaurant after this iconic singer. Together with Marc Cordonnier, he opened Gare au Gorille, a few steps from the St-Lazare station in the booming 17th arrondissement. Initially, their ambition was to run a simple bistro, but the quality of the food that came out of their kitchen attracted foodies from all over the world.

Gare au Gorille is a newcomer that can be traced to Septime. Although this lovely bistro seems somewhat industrial, it has good vibes and energy. A mingling of lots of natural light and well-chosen lighting gives it a very pleasant atmosphere.

Work in the kitchen is taken very seriously. Nothing is accidental and the food is prepared to precision with the very best ingredients. Various textures are handled with utmost intelligence. When you buy the best ingredients, you have to let them do their work.

This is a success story avant la lettre.

HERO

289 Rue Saint-Denis - 75002 Paris
www.quixotic-projects.com/venue/hero
Tue.-Sun. 12.00-14.30 and 19.00-23.00

Korean food, champagne and cool cocktails, a unique combination conceived jointly by the team that has brought us places such as Candelaria, Mary Celeste and Glass.

Yangnyeom

Korean fried chicken

Korean Fried Chicken also known as *yangnyeom tongdak* is already a hit in cities such as London, New York and Berlin and now it looks like the buzz word is Hero in hip Paris. The team came up with this idea during a research trip to Hong Kong with the chef of Mary Celeste. Korean fried chicken means that the French fries are fried twice, just as the Belgians fry them, to guarantee maximum crispiness.

There are two claims to the invention of this world-famous delicacy and two restaurants are fighting for the patent: Pelicana Chicken and Mexican Chicken. Pelicana did introduce yangnyeom tongdak before its competitor, but both use strawberry jam and *gochujang as flavouring.*

Chef Haan Palcu-Chang lived for a long time in Korea and until recently spent his time in the cellar kitchen of Mary Celeste. He is a resolute advocate of the underrated and authentic Korean kitchen with Korean fried chicken serving more or less as an emblematic dish. In collaboration with owner Josh Fontaine, they present a truly tasty menu in addition to the super crispy chicken.

One of their craziest dreams is to one day create a restaurant in a restaurant, a type of Super Hero: there would be only six places for guests inside the kitchen and the chef would be able to go wild upon a simple request of his guests.

But for now, there is only one Hero. The place, located at the corner of Rue d'Aboukir and Rue St-Denis, is already bursting at the seams. The restaurant is on the first floor and offers lots of warmth with its mix of cosy alcoves and bar stools. On the ground floor, cocktails are shaken in sensual Asian style, but what I remember the most is the 'thug life' ("duh").

I don't think it's the ideal place for your first date, but the place is buzzing. The menu is very enticing but – believe me – you want to leave enough room for the rich portions of yangnyeom. This is really a work of art, just a touch of sweetness, very crispy and covered with a spicy garlic sauce or the more piquant *gochujang,* based on Korean chilli.

l'Office

L'OFFICE

3 Rue Richer - 75009 Paris
T +33 1 47 70 67 31
Mon.-Fri. 12.00-14.00 and 19.30-22.30

Little or no decor, with a list of dishes scribbled on a blackboard, and a varied clientele.
Only serve good food and you get a very good Parisian neo-bistro.

Neo-bistro cuisine

The first thing I thought of when entering this place was: the only thing that's missing in Paris is a restaurant with a hunting trophy and several mirrors on the wall. It has an urban woodsman atmosphere, but it is a fantastic place to eat and the décor – or lack of it – doesn't bother the hip crowd at all, on the contrary.

L'Office is a relaxing spot, very popular in the evening among the local hip crowds and during the day frequented by antique dealers from the nearby Drouot Auction House as well as by bankers and business people. And that is a trump card for every restaurant.

Konrad Ceglowski, chef and owner, works according to the tradition of the very best Parisian neo-bistros and offers a market-inspiring modern bistro style that will not leave you indifferent. The subtle dishes are characterised by playfulness and lightness.

L'Office totally blends in with the revival of this neighbourhood, which the locals sometimes call SoPi (South of Pigalle). Delightful businesses spring up here like mushrooms after the rain. This place does have some history as a location of excellent food: the previous owners were all superb chefs. Konrad proves that he has no problem following in the footsteps of his predecessors, which is confirmed by the fact that the place is completely full every day.

TERROIR PARISIEN BOURSE

Palais Brongniart - 25 Place de la Bourse - 75002 Paris
T +33 1 83 92 20 30 - www.yannick-alleno.com
Mon.-Fri. 12.00-15.00 and 19.00-23.00

Yannick Alléno is one of a few chef superstars. He is mainly well-known for his 10-year stint
as a chef in the famous Le Meurice where in merely three years he managed to cook up three
stars for this restaurant. 'The prince of the palace' became his nickname.

Charcuterie

RILLETTES

Alléno introduces a kitchen considered by many to be a form of art. He has a gift for reinventing classics by looking at them from an entirely different angle, similar to what Warhol did with his silk-screen prints. "Images, multiply them with silk-screening, see them with a different feeling,' wrote Lou Reed about Warhol's vision, and this description applies to Alléno's work. Local products inspire him and connect the classic to the modern. Alléno has a strong culinary identity and a great personality. He is a perfectionist in every sense of the word, and he is more than happy to attempt pioneering work. He enjoys demonstrating his exceptional talent in many restaurants that he is affiliated with, but he has opened a small chain of restaurants in Paris which he calls Terroir Parisien.

Have you ever been to a rillette bar? In his Terroir Parisien, Alléno pays tribute to simplicity, to the real common kitchen, the kitchens of the brasseries and bistros. The dishes that we eat while chatting over a glass of beer. Pâté and toasted bread, Parisian ham, liverwurst, sweetbread sausages, leeks vinaigrette, wonderful bread, and of course a rich selection of various types of rillettes that you will find in a rillette bar.

The restaurant is somewhat hidden, deep below the stately Palais Brongniart, but it is really worth coming here to taste the lovely local dishes, seen through the eyes of a culinary superstar.

ADDITIONAL EATERIES
MONTMARTRE / GRANDS BOULEVARDS / PLACE DE CLICHY / PIGALLE

ABRI
92 Rue du Faubourg Poissonnière, 75010 Paris
T +33 1 83 97 00 00
Mon. 12.00-15.00; Thu.-Fri. 12.30-14.00 and 20.00-22.00;
Sat. 12.30-15.00 and 19.30-22.00

ATAO
86 Rue Lemercier, 75017 Paris
T +33 1 46 27 81 12
Thu.-Sun. 12.30-14.30 and 19.30-23.00

AU CAMION QUI FUME
168 Rue Montmartre, 75002 Paris
T +33 1 84 16 33 75
www.lecamionquifume.com
Sun.-Thu. 11.00-23.00; Fri.-Sat. 11.00-00.00

IL BRIGANTE
4 Rue du Ruisseau, 75018 Paris
T +33 1 44 92 72 15
Mon.-Sat. 12.00-14.30 and 19.30-23.30

LA CAVE DE GASTON LEROUX
106 Rue Lepic, 75018 Paris
T +33 1 42 64 42 97

LE PANTRUCHE
3 Rue Victor Masse, 75009 Paris
T +33 1 48 78 55 60
Mon.-Fri. 12.30-14.30 and 19.30-22.30

LE PETIT BLEU
23 Rue Muller, 75018 Paris
T +33 1 42 59 27 01
Mon.-Sat. 12.00-15.00 and 19.00-23.30

PECO PECO
47 Rue Jean-Baptiste Pigalle, 75009 Paris
T +33 1 53 16 19 84
Thu.-Sat. 12.00-14.00 and 19.00-22.00

PLEINE MER
22 Rue de Chabrol, 75010 Paris
T +33 1 53 34 64 47
Thu.-Sat. 10.30-15.00 and 16.00-23.30

CLAMATO

80 Rue de Charonne - 75011 Paris
T +33 1 43 72 74 53 - www.septime-charonne.fr
Wed.-Fri. 19.00-23.00; Sat.-Sun. 12.00-23.00

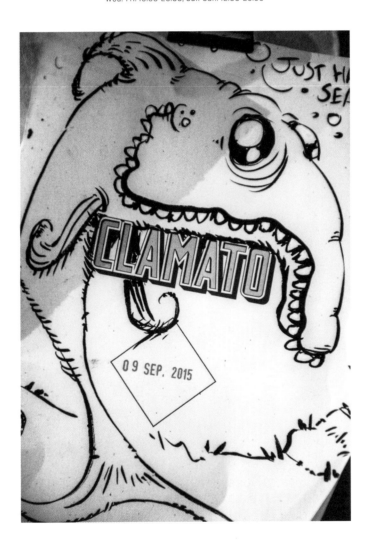

Have you ever eaten jellyfish? I eat it frequently in the better Japanese and Chinese restaurants. It has a unique bite and when prepared properly, it is very tasty.

Céviche

Seasoned and marinated raw fish & seafood

You might wrinkle you nose and swear that you would never touch it, but statistics show that after 2050, jellyfish will be the only seafood to be fished from the ocean. Sorry to disappoint you.

This shocking thought did not dissuade Bertrand Grébaut from opening Clamato, a few doors away from his Septime restaurant. Clamato became an oyster and seafood bar of the highest order. The only concession to international trends is the somewhat atypical name, which literally means tomato juice made with clam broth. In Canada, the tomato juice of the Bloody Mary is replaced with clamato to create a Bloody Caesar, although most American barmen are convinced that you can only make a good Bloody Mary by adding a certain proportion of clamato.

Sea and the City must be the concept that Bertrand and Theo had in mind. Just like Septime, this gem of a restaurant is dead on target. The architects Guillaume Jounet and Remy Bardin from Hold Up Architecture chose raw minimalism in its cosy design. Beer garden tables were the favoured design objects given the right surroundings and colours. But I assume that the popularity of this restaurant does not depend on its subtle interior design. Most of the time it is so packed that the crowd blocks the view of the design. In a place where the food is self-explanatory, that's no problem. People clearly come here to enjoy Bertrand's beautiful and harmonious kitchen and his talent for preparing oysters, sea urchins, meagre and anything else delicious that he can find.

Clamato is a tribute to the sea in all respects. Since my youth, I have always been fascinated by the sea, so for me this is an address to frequent often. I even surprise myself when I walk right past Septime to Clamato without noticing. That is clear proof that Clamato works!

CLOWN BAR

114 Rue Amelot - 75011 Paris
T +33 1 43 55 87 35 - www.clown-bar-paris.fr
Wed.-Sun. 12.00-14.30 and 19.00-22.30

There is something magical about this oval-shaped building with its twenty sides.
It is the historical Cirque d'Hiver on Rue Amelot.

GRIMALDI

Pigeon

On December 11, 1852, Napoleon III was here in order to officially open the Cirque Napoléon, as it was then called. In 1870, the building was rechristened Cirque d'Hiver.

Whenever we think of a clown, what usually comes to mind is the familiar Auguste. This figure with the typical make up – the striking red nose, the gigantic shoes and the colourful clothing – is inextricably connected to our childhood. Incidentally, a clown not only makes children laugh, but also young and old people. Joseph Grimaldi, the first clown, is the person we must thank for bringing us this figure. He introduced this role during the harlequinade that his classical British pantomime group created at the Théatre Royal, Covent Garden and Sadler's Wells in London. This type of clown became known by the nickname Joey and is still called that way in the English-speaking world. The English word 'clown' actually emerged far earlier and was used for the first time in 1560, when it became a synonym for a farmer. In that sense, Shakespeare also used the term clown in *Othello* and in *A Winter's Tale*. In 17th century England, the harlequinade developed, inspired by the classical Italian Commedia dell'arte and

that's how the clown has evolved into its current form.

Clowns too have to eat and that's why we are now going to visit a restaurant where you cannot have coulrophobia – a fear of clowns. Adjacent to the monumental Cirque d'Hiver was a dark tobacco-stained communal canteen where the clowns used to eat. After thoroughly cleaning the old canteen, the true nature of the place emerged: beautiful hand-painted circus and clown figures and themes on glass and tiles as well as the bar where Toulouse-Lautrec would come to have a drink.

The Clown Bar has developed into a concept, one of the best bistros in Paris with a dream team to match it. Sven Chartier and Ewen Lemoigne (Saturne) combined with Xavier Lacaud and the Japanese chef, Sota Atsumi, in the kitchen guarantees fireworks at all levels.

The kitchen is of a very high standard and makes many a starred-chef blush, while the wine list, the speciality of Xavier (aka Mr X), is an example of what a modern wine list should look like.

Superb!

FRENCHIE

5 Rue du Nil - 75002 Paris
T +33 1 40 39 96 19 - www.frenchie-restaurant.com
Mon.-Fri. 18.30-22.00

Whenever I walk along the super hip Rue du Nil, I ask myself why they don't just change its name to Rue du Frenchie, because it seems as if Gregory Marchand has this street all to himself.

Menu carte blanche

There's Frenchie, Frenchie to go, Frenchie caviste, Frenchie bar à vins and I've probably overlooked a few others... Well, we have to admit, this 'Rue du Frenchie' is a lovely and attractive street where everything is focused on good food and drinks... thanks to Gregory Marchand.

When Gregory worked at Fifteen in Shoreditch – one of the Jamie Oliver's projects – Jamie came up with the nickname Frenchie for him. That's why it was so obvious that Gregory would use this name for the restaurant he opened in 2009. Initially, he stood all by himself in the kitchen with one staff member in the dining room. But this situation proved to be dead on target, something that master chefs could only dream of. Was it the combination of a relaxed atmosphere, the extensive international wine list and the amazing dishes? No one knows for sure. But now that Gregory has opened a restaurant in Covent Garden in London, it looks like he's come full circle.

Frenchie is the type of restaurant where Greg himself would come to dine. His dishes are deeply rooted in the classic French kitchen, but they have also acquired an international tone that originates from global inspiration. Gregory originally comes from Nantes, but did not have many reasons for remaining in France. He worked in New York at the world-famous Gramercy Tavern, in Hong Kong, in Spain and as already mentioned, in London. As a matter of fact, he was doing a shift in Gramercy Tavern when he received the wonderful news that he was to become a father. He immediately decided to return to France and that's how the name Frenchie was conceived.

From day one, when Frenchie stood alone in this charming bistro district, Gregory's kitchen surprised friends and foes. Moreover, the food was top quality while the prices stayed reasonable. He could not have imagined how much influence his bistro would have and that he was introducing a new culinary style in Paris.

Frenchie became such a feel good place; when the taxi comes to pick me up and drives slowly into the night while there are still guests sitting there and eating, I feel I'm missing out on something, a bit like a child who has to go to bed early.

JONES

43 Rue Godefroy Cavaignac - 75011 Paris
T +33 9 80 75 32 08 - www.jonescaferestaurant.com
Mon.-Sun. 18.00-02.00

Sitting on the dock of the bay reverberates from the speakers of this cross between an industrial loft and an alternative concert hall.

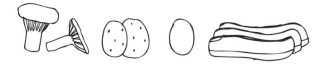

Chanterelle mushrooms, potatoes, egg and bacon

This very pleasant *bar à manger* (food bar) has an incredible vibe that reminds me immediately of the relaxed atmosphere in Haight-Ashbury in San Francisco.

It was previously called Jones Bones. At the end of 2015, the Australian autodidactic chef, James Henry, closed Bones and Florent Ciccoli took the occasion of the New Year to transform Bones into Jones. The space remained more or less the same and still has that raw mystery that makes this spot so attractive.

The cuisine of Florent, who used to work in Bones (but not in the kitchen), is exceptionally pertinent.

Florent has found his way into the kitchen and discovered himself as a chef who prefers working with seasonal products, combining them in a surprising way. The food is served on small plates with items from the kitchen that will guarantee a nice and tasty evening.

Here you can feel the vibes of the staff who enjoy what they do and are happy that their guests continue to appreciate Jones. *'L'homme n'a pas besoin de voyager pour s'agrandir, il porte en lui l'immensité.'* ('Mankind does not need to travel to get bigger: he carries immensity within him.')

A keeper!

LA TABLE D'HUGO DESNOYER À LA HALLE SECRÉTAN

33 avenue Secrétan - 75019 Paris
T +33 1 40 05 10 79 - www.hugodesnoyer.com

Tue.-Sat. afternoon and evening

Since 1868, la Halle or le Marché Secrétan has been an integral part of the street scenery on Avenue Secrétan. The building was designed by Victor Baltard and the Polonceau style metal trusses catch the eye in particular. The significance of la Halle was further emphasised in 1982 when it was placed on the list of historical monuments.

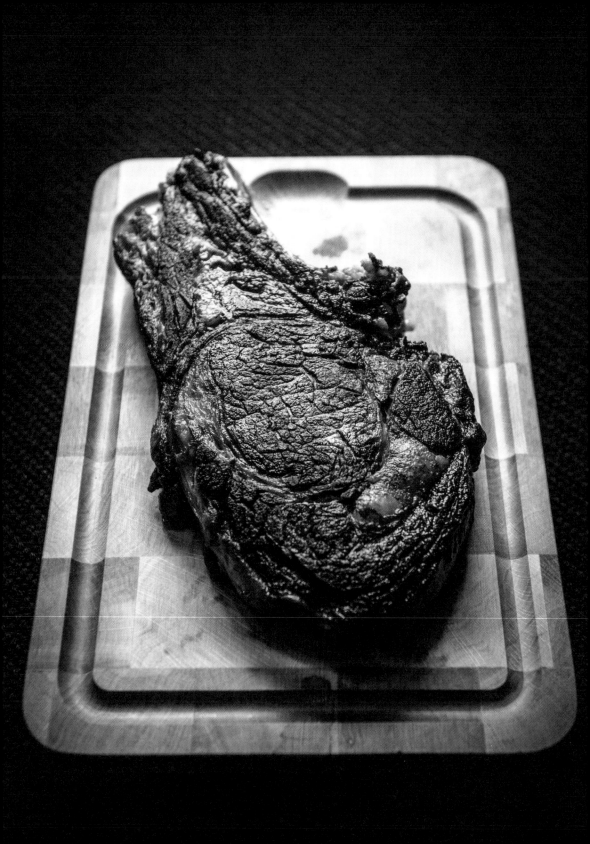

Rib steak

Hugo Desnoyer is one the most prominent butchers in France. By now, his name and fame reach all the way to Japan. The young Hugo never made an effort in school, but when he turned sixteen something fundamental changed in the adolescent rebel. During his apprenticeship at an inspiring butcher, he discovered his passion and calling.

He totally fell under the spell of the artisanal craftsmen who were happy to teach the young and inquisitive Hugo everything about the trade. He amassed a great deal of knowledge and learned to display precision alongside tough discipline. Nowadays, he is one of the most fanatic advocates of this traditional trade.

His vision nevertheless is very simple: to offer customers the best product that can be found. He scouts all the corners of France looking for the best breeders, the best-looking animals, bred with care and raised in a natural environment.

He has a real gift for the trade; he is a sort of cattle whisperer. And that does not go unnoticed. He supplies distinguished chefs, the best restaurants and anyone who loves excellent meat. He speaks of meat as someone else might speak of poetry and it's not uncommon to find celebrities such as Carla Bruni and Cathérine Deneuve standing next to you at the counter of his boucherie.

Dining at one of Hugo's restaurants is a meat paradise. His innovation is evident by the fact that his cuts are not classified by the breed or hanging time, but rather by taste, so that the guest immediately knows what to order. The meat ranges from a delicate taste to a hearty taste with a pronounced structure.

The restaurant is the result of a friendship between four people: eyewear guru Alain Mikli whose unique line of eyeglasses has contributed to the looks of Andy Warhol, Elton John and Jeanne Moreau, to name a few. But above all, he is Hugo's business angel; architect Imaad Rahmouni who is an old friend of Hugo; chef Frédéric Chabbert; and Hugo himself. All four were enamoured by the charm of la Halle Secrétan, so there was no stopping them.

It is always a pleasure to rub shoulders with such ambitious and talented people; you feel the vibe penetrating through the cowhides. A must for meat lovers.

LE MAZENAY

46 Rue de Montmorency - 75003 Paris
T +33 6 42 83 79 52 - www.lemazenay.com
Thu.-Fri. 12.00-15.00 and 19.00-23.00; Sat. 19.00-23.00

Denis Groison is my hero! He was born in the little village of Mazenay in Bourgogne and thus
the name of the restaurant, Le Mazenay. And what a place. On a quiet street, this modern
attractive premise hits the mark.

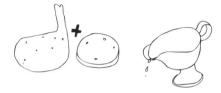

Pigeon with goose liver, mustard sauce, spiced spring vegetables

Denis is the chef and owner and has more than fifteen years of experience in haute gastronomy. He also became internationally known because after his stint at Guy Lassausaie (two stars in Lyons) he became a chef at The Raffles in Singapore and at the Metropole in Hanoi, remaining a fervent follower of classical French cuisine which doesn't leave much room for creativity. In 2013, he opened his first restaurant in the heart of Puces de St-Ouen, but a few months later he moved to Le Mazenay, where he continued to study the purity of dishes. Denis is a chef full of passion who lives for his products and his dishes.

A good illustration is the dish of perfectly prepared dove combined with top-quality foie gras and an amazing sauce. A Last-Supper dish that is unparalleled.

This new gem, a stone's throw from Beaubourg, is a real addition, certainly for lovers of French cuisine, without a big crowd and fanfare. This cuisine is straightforward, yet with every bite, you taste the immense talent of its excellent chef.

Incidentally, Denis originates from a family of bakers. He demonstrates this with an exceptionally wonderful family dish, the Millefeuille (cake of a thousand sheets) with rum cream – a real feast, more so because the Millefeuille is his father's recipe and the cream comes from his grandfather. There is no finer family tradition than this.

AU COMPTOIR...
- Rillettes de cochon 5€
- Saucisson de l'Ardèche 7€
- TERRINES Du MOMENT de 9 à 12€

AU COMPTOIR
- Olives noires de kalamata 3
- Radis beurre
- œuf dur, mayonnaise à l'oseille 3€
- Soupette 1€

LE REPAIRE DE CARTOUCHE

8 Boulevard des Filles du Calvaire - 75011 Paris
T +33 1 47 00 25 86
Mon. 12.00-14.30; Thu.-Sat. 12.00-14.30 and 19.30-23.00; Sun. 12.00-15.00

Rodolphe Paquin, the very impressive owner and manager of what used to be a dark robber's den, is a very gifted chef who does everything possible to continue working in a traditional manner. But who is, or more correctly, was, Cartouche?

Pâté en croûte

a Parisian monument

Louis-Dominique Cartouche was a famous Parisian, born in October 1693. After leaving his home on 19 Rue du Pont-aux-Choux at the age of twelve, he spent his teens cheating and stealing and eventually landed in the military. Although he turned out to be a brave and intelligent soldier, the free-rolling life in the streets of Paris enticed him much more. He deserted and hid in Rue Amelot. He surrounded himself with a group of bad guys and soon became the leader of a gang of more than 200 members, specialising in theft and ambushes in the Parisian suburbs.

Thanks to the many friends he made during his military career, who later helped him avoid the clutches of the police, he was able to start making something of his life. Sadly, however, one of his trusted lieutenants betrayed him and on the 27 November 1721 Cartouche was hung, drawn and quartered.

By his 28th birthday, he had become a real folk hero.

Cartouche led his congenial life from this restaurant on the Rue Amelot, where his presence lingers in the wall paintings that portray his decadent life.

Rodolphe himself is also a folk hero, a free-roller who can count on a great deal of sympathy and admiration from his regular, trusted clientele. In any case, he certainly has my absolute admiration. This is a restaurant that makes you feel at home no matter what you eat, because everything here is unbelievably tasty and traditionally prepared.

To enjoy his various patés and terrines, the subject of his recent book, I would be happy to walk several kilometres. This is one of the Parisian monuments that you will not find on a tourist map.

LE VERRE VOLÉ

67 Rue de Lancry - 75010 Paris
T +33 1 48 03 17 34 - www.leverrevole.fr
Daily 12.00-14.30 and 19.30-23.30

At first glance, Le Verre Volé looks like a run-of-the-mill wine shop.
But when you reserve a spot, if you manage to do so, you soon realise that this
is a place of pilgrimage, a real cult wine bar.

Menu of the day

Wine is the main attraction here, especially unfiltered natural wine. Le Verre Volé is one of the pioneers of this major transition experienced by the wine world. The trendy neighbourhood on the Canal St-Martin is the ideal decor for a top wine bar such as this one. Le Verre Volé has three locations in Paris, but only this one is suitable for a real lunch or dinner. And don't forget: reservation is an absolute must, because there are only a limited number of places. In London or New York, you would be standing in a queue that goes around the block for this type of bar.

Le Verre Volé does much of its business as a wine shop. You simply choose the bottle you want. They charge an additional 7 euros for corkage. While you're eating, it's not uncommon to see someone park his motor scooter next to the front door and squeeze in between the diners in order to buy his favourite wine.

The kitchen looks like it was built for a submarine, yet the dishes conjured up and served from this tiny place are magnificent. What is it about this mythical place? Is it the gentle anarchy that reigns here, the temptation of the dishes scribbled on a large chalkboard, the organised chaos that dominates? Is it the charisma of Cyril Bordarier that ensures that all lovers of fine wine find their way to Le Verre Volé? Who knows? One thing is for sure: it is a one-of-a-kind wine bar. If you type in Google 'bar à vin Paris' (Parisian wine bar), a photo of Le Verre Volé will definitely appear on the screen. A textbook example of how it should be and how someone in his most romantic dreams would imagine what the ideal French wine bar in Paris would look like.

MARCHÉ DES ENFANTS ROUGES

39 Rue de Bretagne - 75003 Paris
Tue.-Sun. the market is closed from 13.00 to 16.00, but the food stalls are open

What can be more fun than a local market where you can buy all the necessary qualitative ingredients for cooking a cosy meal at home, but where you can also sit and enjoy wonderful food?

Bento

I can't visit London without going to Borough Market, nor can I walk past the Boqueria in Barcelona, even if I have just eaten.

Rue de Bretagne is one of my favourite streets, because that's where I find samplings of what France has to offer in the way of top-quality ingredients. Here you will find poulterers, butchers, bakers, charcutiers, fishmongers... it's difficult to resist them all.

This street is also home to the Marché des Enfants Rouges (Market of the Red Children), the oldest covered market in Paris where foodstuffs have been traded daily since 1628. Originally, this market was called Le Petit Marché du Marais but it takes its current name from the former hospice des Enfants-Rouges which was established for the city's orphans by Marguerite de Navarre, who dressed the children in red uniforms, hence its name. When the hospice closed in 1777, the market was named after it. Since March 8, 1982, the market has been on the list of national historical monuments.

This place is certainly equipped to fight the hungriest of stomachs. Feel like Lebanese, Italian, African or perhaps Japanese? The chaotic atmosphere so characteristic of such a market is what makes it so irresistible. All the food stalls do their best to organise some sort of sitting arrangements to make their guests as comfortable as possible in this chaotic, but nice bustle. Just next to the market is a mini vegetable garden, the Jardin des Oiseaux. This is a lovely urban gardening project of the neighbourhood residents. Apparently, the spot of the garden was formerly a place where cows were kept to provide the residents with a constant supply of fresh milk.

For me, this market and the entire Rue de Bretagne is an ideal address for brunch and lunch.

LA SOCULENTE

MIZNON

22 Rue des Ecouffes - 75004 Paris
T +33 1 42 74 83 58
Sun.-Thu. 12.00-23.30; Fri. 12.00-16.00

If you are walking along Rue des Ecouffes and notice a restaurant that's so busy
that it looks like a Boxing Day sale at Harrods, you can almost be certain that
it's Miznon, where everyone wants to be.

Cauliflower

The headquarters of Miznon is in Tel Aviv. Although the interior design is very simple, it has enormous appeal. Is it because of the items scrawled on the chalkboard that looks like a cross between graffiti and grottos of Lascaux? For me, it is the modest shelf with whole roasted cauliflowers. This is the world-famous dish that every famous TV cook has already presented and every stylish food critic has covered in the last year.

Why has this roasted and charred cauliflower taken the culinary world by storm?

Every famous and hyped dish has to begin somewhere. This one was created around ten years ago by the famous Israeli chef, Eyal Shani. The dish rapidly attained god-like status in his North Abraxas restaurant. Eyal and his wife, Miri Hanoch, worked together on a weekly food column and their cauliflower adventures appeared there between 2006 and 2009. Since then, this cauliflower has been conquering the foodie world and started a rediscovery of general Israeli food in the US. The first to go along in the US was Alon Shaya, who has a modern Israeli restaurant in New Orleans. The dam ultimately burst when Jamie Oliver immortalized the dish.

So what's the story behind this cauliflower that looks charred on top? Shani has long been a well-known authority on the Israeli culinary scene. He has

nine restaurants of which seven are located in Israel, including the famous North Abraxas. His international gourmet pita chain, Miznon, has five branches: three in Tel Aviv, one in Vienna and of course this one in Paris.

One Friday evening, Shani was visiting his partner, Shahar Segal, I order to eat a home-made meal together. The hungry Shani asked what was cooking and opened the oven door. There they were in full glory, small cauliflowers, roasted whole with a black charred finish. Shani was immediately jealous. As a lover of cauliflower, why didn't he think of this dish?

It's my mother's recipe, confessed Shahar. The recipe is ridiculously simple and you need so few ingredients: a small cauliflower and olive oil, that's it! The trick is to apply the olive oil with your hands so that you don't overlook any spot. Otherwise it doesn't work, says Shahar.

While the hustle and bustle at Miznon continues, through the window I see a long queue of tourists across the street waiting for some dime-a-dozen pita bread – and I ask myself why on earth? I'd rather be here in this industrial chic pita bar watching the many cooks making stuffed pita sandwiches from scratch in the open kitchen using top-notch ingredients. Wait patiently for your name to be called and then, in a few minutes, you will be in seventh heaven.

營業中

Chère Clientèle
Tous nos plats contiennent du porc.

Dear Customers
All our ramen broths contain pork.

NARITAKE RAMEN

31 Rue des Petits Champs - 75001 Paris
T +33 1 42 86 03 83
Mon.-Sat. 11.30-15.00 and 18.30-22.00

In the Japanese quarter of Paris, near the monumental opera house, you will find many Ramen restaurants. But which is the best one to visit?

Ramen

Ramen expert Hiroshi Osaki claims that the very first Ramen eatery opened in 1910 in Yokohama, although the origin of the dish is not that clear. Certain sources say that the roots of this hearty dish are in China, others, like Osaki, say Japan.

What is certain is that this dish has truly conquered the world and that the name is the Japanese pronunciation of the Chinese *lamian*. Until the 1950s, Ramen in Japan was called *shinasoba; chukasoba*, or simply Ramen, are now more accepted as common names. According to tradition, this dish was made popular by Chinese labourers in Japan who usually sold the boiled noodles in meat broths, sometimes with *gyoza* in them. Ramen also became popular because of the typical music played by the street vendors to announce their arrival, the *charumera*, derived from the Portuguese *charamela*.

But the real advance came after WW2 when many soldiers returned from China, where they had enjoyed eating their delicious Ramen on a daily basis. Moreover, masses of cheap American flour were available on the Japanese market, for obvious reasons.

In addition, in 1958 a certain Momofuku Ando developed something that would change the world: instant noodles. At that time, Ando was running Nissin Foods. These instant Ramen, as they were sometimes called, were the biggest Japanese invention of the 20th century. Of course, the only thing that was missing – and was established in 1994 in Yokohama – was a Ramen Museum.

All this is just to let you know that the Ramen at Naritake Ramen is the best in all of Paris. The Miso Ramen, originally a regional dish from Hokkaido, is truly phenomenal. The bouillon here is thick and tasty and can compete with any real Japanese experience. I would really like to know what Ivan Orkin, the Ramen specialist, thinks of it. Don't be discouraged by the sometimes long queue outside. This Ramen is simply worth waiting for.

OBER MAMMA

107 Boulevard Richard Lenoir - 75011 Paris
T +33 1 58 30 62 78 - www.bigmammagroup.com/ober-mamma
Mon.-Fri. 12.15-14.15 and 19.00-22.45; Sat.-Sun. 12.15-15.30 and 19.00-23.00

There are very few dishes that illustrate the simplicity of the Italian kitchen as clearly as *pasta carbonara*. How do you make a more than superlative dish with almost no ingredients?

Pasta carbonara

The origins of this dish are not that clear, as is often the case with dishes that originate in family traditions. Rome lays claim to this dish, but there are many other competitors.

Here is a bit of history for you. In 1839, Ippolito Cavalcanti wrote the influential cookbook, *Cucina teorico-practica*, which contained a recipe for pasta with eggs and cheese. In 1912, a miner, Federico Salomone, opened the restaurant La Carbonara in Rome. Although it makes no claim to this dish, this restaurant does prepare it and according to the Italian food and wine magazine, Gambero Rosso, they make a version that's considered among the top ten in Italy. Of course there is also the influence of the American soldiers during World War II, who mixed bacon and eggs into their pasta. The soldiers arrived in Rome in 1944, but only since 1951 has the dish *pasta alla carbonara* emerged as such in Italian culinary writings.

It seems very unlikely that the dish originated from the miners *(carbonari)*. As soon as the dish became popular, people no longer referred the name *carbonara* to miners in the vernacular, but to a secret Napoleonic freemason fraternity, which in turn based the name on a similar Scottish fraternity from the 15th century.

Be that as it may, a well-prepared pasta carbonara is a great classic dish, even though it has not existed for long. And in Ober Mamma you can eat a more than fantastic version of it.

Tigrane Seydoux and Victor Lugger are two friends who are in love with Italy and especially with Italian cooking. Ober Mamma and their other establishment, Big Mamma, are a tribute to Italy and to the small *trattorias* and *osterias* where their parents took them when they were kids – and where later they took their own loved ones. The two partners visited countless agricultural businesses, always looking for that one special product. Their aim was to make the trattoria a popular and common eating place, just like in Italy. They make absolutely no compromises on the quality of the products and ingredients, just like Luigi Romolo in Naples and Giuseppe Zen in Milan.

Ober Mamma, close to the Oberkampf underground station, is an impressive, dynamic establishment where all sorts of things are going on and where age-long pure Italian chaos reigns, but which is actually not real chaos. It is truly different here; an open kitchen in the middle of the restaurant, a wood pizza oven in the shape of a big barrel, a 5000-litre stainless steel tank of olive oil. A designer was given a free hand here to bestow a sense of freedom upon the building. Martin Brudnizki designs most of the Jamie Oliver restaurants as well as many houses in Soho, and in spite of the monumental character of this establishment, he has retained the low threshold character of a common trattoria. *Forza Italia!*

SEPTIME

80 Rue de Charonne - 75011 Paris
T +33 1 43 67 38 29 - www.septime-charonne.fr
Tue.-Fri. 12.15-14.00 and 19.30-22.00; Mon. 19.30-22.00

Why is it that every time I enter Septime, I unavoidably think of the *Birth of the Cool* of Miles Davis? The album symbolises the moment that Miles abandoned the almost aggressive up-tempo of the bebop and pioneered a sultrier and softer style, which ultimately became an important chapter in the evolution of jazz.

Flavourful market cuisine

Septime attracts the cool crowd with all its pros and cons. When Bertrand Grebaut, the ambitious magical student of Alain Passard, opened this beautiful and relaxed neo-bistro, he had no idea that it would surpass his wildest dreams. Septime became a statement and since then a culinary guide of Paris that doesn't include this establishment would be unthinkable. Incidentally, the name Septime is a tribute to Monsieur Septime, the main character from *Le Grand Restaurant*, the cult gastro-comedy with Louis de Funès.

Septime is what it is: only premium ingredients get access to the kitchen, Jimmy Hendrix's best blues repertoire sounds from the loudspeakers and the guests around you are food industry pros and globe-trotting foodies.

Bertrand and his partner, Théo Pourriat, have thought about every detail and made the smart move to leave sufficient room for improvisation. Bertrand is a late-bloomer in the kitchen. He first studied literature at university

and only much later, he succumbed to his passion for cooking. He wanted to release the French kitchen from the super deluxe hotels and restaurants and show that fantastic food can be enjoyed in a simple setting. Bertrand describes his own cooking style as naive, spontaneous and balanced. For me, his kitchen evokes an awakening sensuality, as Colette wrote in her 1923 novel, *Le blé en herbe*.

Since Chateaubriand introduced very limited menus and the obligatory menu formula, this has more or less become the standard in Paris of what is totally hip, trendy and hot. If Chateaubriand is the pioneer of these formulas, then Septime is the perfect catalyst and no one challenges this role.

Septime is no doubt one of the best restaurants in Paris, and it's difficult to get a table. But you must persist, no matter how many times you have to press the redial button on your phone. Once you're there, you'll think of only one thing: how and when do I return as quickly as possible!

PLACE DE LA BASTILLE / PLACE DE LA RÉPUBLIQUE / LE MARAIS

TABLE

3 Rue de Prague - 75012 Paris
T +33 1 43 43 12 26 - www.tablerestaurant.fr
Mon.-Fri. 12.00-14.00 and 19.30-22.00; Sat. 19.30-23.00

TABLE

137

PLACE DE LA BASTILLE / PLACE DE LA RÉPUBLIQUE / LE MARAIS

In an era where many chefs promote pure cuisine, it's a true breath of fresh air to encounter someone who really understands what this entails and live up to this principle. A cuisine of real products without frills, but rather with a genuine philosophy rooted in deep emotions and contemplations and no hip concept that responds to a momentary trend.

Foie gras

Bruno Verjus was born and raised in Renaison, near Roanne. He comes from a generation that considered milk from the farm cows, chickens that an aunt brought over and freshly-picked fruit and vegetables to be the most normal way of life. The young Bruno considered becoming a doctor, but eventually decided to study marketing and travelled throughout the world. Bruno, however, only saw the light after meeting Pierre Hermé at the beginning of the 1990s.

His passion for the kitchen and its flavours led him to sell his business in 2005 in order to excel in cooking. Like a devout monk, he devoted himself full-time to this pursuit. In his blog, Food Intelligence, Bruno tells inquisitive readers about his encounters with artisanal producers and shares his culinary experiences. He starts by posing frantic questions about the most proper methods of processing and preparing a certain product. His kitchen soul mate, Alain Passard, is there to support him.

Whether he is in Paris or at his beloved Île d'Yeu, the rural customs of his childhood never abandon him. The distance between the artisanal producer and the diner sitting in front of the dish must be as short as possible.

But the poacher became a hunter and the culinary reviewer became a chef at an age when most chefs think of retiring. In April 2013, Table became a fact. Table is a place where artisanal products are the most natural thing in the world, and are handled in the most respectful manner and served up to the guests. The restaurant looks very different from most restaurants and although ironically named the Table, its tables are not really tables in the strict sense of the word. The interior slightly reminds me of a top sushi bar, not because of the food, but because of the intimate relationship between the guest and the chef. Everyone sits down at a sort of airplane wing, a bit like the way Anselm Kiefer exhibits this in some of his monumental sculptures. The kitchen is completely open and transparent and the workers encounter the guests at frequent moments, engaging in intimate dialogue.

Bruno's cuisine is pure, simple and accepts only the very best ingredients, meticulously observed so that the cooks can make the best of both their qualities and their faults. The dishes are designed so that each bite is different. Each dish has its own history. It is up to the guest to discover the subtleties; to read between the lines and discover the nuances that Bruno has captured. This can only be achieved by intensive contact with the suppliers.

The motto is "Start every day from scratch" while a 1.8 kg piece of sole lies in clarified butter. The cooling is a treasure chest with the best that France can offer, and believe me – you taste it! Out of respect for animal life, animals must be properly prepared and that can only be done if you love them.

A piece of foie gras gazes at me and finds its way to my mouth. Hopeless. No manipulations to disguise the taste. Simply pure goose liver braised whole and then, after cooling, cut like a terrine. Salt, pepper and cacao constitute the decor. Incredibly poignant how it goes hand in hand with homemade bread, the type that many top bakers would give their right arm for.

Pure. Purer. Bruno Verjus.

TABLE

139

PLACE DE LA BASTILLE / PLACE DE LA RÉPUBLIQUE / LE MARAIS

THE BEAST

PICK-UP

ORDER

Today's Special
Smoked Pastrami
Sauerkraut
17 €

DECK & DONOHUE
The Beast
11/3

BEAST

Today's Special
Smoked Pastrami &
Sauerkraut
17 €

THE BEAST

27 Rue Meslay - 75003 Paris
T +33 7 81 02 99 77
Tue.-Sat. 12.00-14.30 and 19.00-23.00

Thomas Abramowicz had a successful marketing career in the luxury industry. That was until he began to ponder the meaning of life, and his own path in particular, and decided to take an entirely different course.

Texas barbecue

In New York City he had an "aha" moment when he ate at one of the best barbecue restaurants in the city: Fette Sau. Thomas didn't need to look any further! He became infatuated with the genuine Texas-style barbecue and asked Wayne Mueller to mentor him on it. He was willing to do anything, even start as a dishwasher. Wayne agreed to cooperate and initiated Thomas into the secrets of the smoker.

Louie Mueller is a genuine concept when it comes to the Texas barbecue. He initially arrived in Texas in 1936 to open a grocery store and in 1949 he opened this barbecue restaurant. Wayne Mueller currently runs the barbecue in Fette Sau. Their visiting card is the beef brisket and this is the same at The Beast.

Thomas is clearly someone who leaves nothing to chance. He equipped The Beast with a heavy two-ton smoker made in Mesquite, Texas. It runs 24/7 at full blast and is fed with French oak only. During the night, the selected meat is smoked slowly to perfection and absorbs the distinct smoky taste that makes it irresistible. In the evening the meat is preserved and served for lunch the next day.

The result is incredible and for someone like me, who has spent years in the US and is a regular at Fette Sau, it is astounding. The meat is as smooth as butter, perfectly cooked, with just the right smoky taste that makes this style of barbequing so enticing. The range is completely to the point – brisket, beef sausage, ribs and pastrami... all authentically made and insanely delicious. Just as sushi makes me homesick for Tokyo, this restaurant gives a coming home feeling to anyone who has ever eaten in a barbecue joint in the US.

Finding the right meat was no easy feat, because French cattle are leaner than their US cousins. Meat, fire and time are a way of life for pit-master Thomas. Follow the typical subtle aroma when you're walking along Rue Meslay and you will reach the place without any problem. And don't forget the rich selection of bourbons, which will remind you of the other side of the ocean.

To complete the atmosphere, an authentic Stars & Stripes hangs at a place of honour in Thomas's restaurant. When the meat was ready at Wayne Mueller, the flag was raised. If there was no brisket left, the flag was lowered and folded up. That way, passer-bys could decide whether or not to go in if what they had in mind was the brisket. This flag, which Thomas received as a gift when he opened The Beast, has loyally done its duty for years in Texas.

ADDITIONAL EATERIES
PLACE DE LA BASTILLE / PLACE DE LA RÉPUBLIQUE / LE MARAIS

BALLS
47 Rue Saint-Maur, 75011 Paris
T +33 9 51 38 74 89
Thu.-Sat. 12.00-14.30 and 19.30-22.30

BREIZH CAFÉ
109 Rue Vieille du Temple, 75003 Paris
T +33 1 42 72 13 77
www.breizhcafe.com/fr
Wed.-Sat. 11.30-23.00; Sun. 11.30-22.00

CHEZ BOBOSSE – LE QUINCY
28 Avenue Ledru-Rollin, 75012 Paris
T +33 1 46 28 46 76
www.lequincy.fr

CHEZ RAMONA
17 Rue Ramponeau, 75020 Paris
T +33 1 46 36 83 55
Thu.-Sun. 14.00-02.00

COME A CASA
7 Rue Pache, 75011 Paris
T +33 1 77 15 08 19
www.comeacasa7.tumblr.com
Mon.-Sat. 12.00-15.00 and 19.00-22.00

DAILY SYRIEN
55 Rue du Faubourg Saint-Denis, 75010 Paris
T +33 9 54 11 75 35
Sun.-Mon. 11.30-20.00; Thu.-Sat. 11.30-00.00

DERSOU
21 Rue Saint-Nicolas, 75012 Paris
T +33 9 81 01 12 73
www.dersouparis.com
Thu.-Fri. 19.30-00.00; Sat. 12.00-15.30 and 19.30-00.00;
Sun. 12.00-15.30

DÜO
24 Rue du Marché Popincourt, 75011 Paris
T +33 9 82 49 43 63
Thu.-Sat. 12.00-23.00; Sun. 12.00-18.00

JAMBO
23 Rue Sainte-Marthe, 75010 Paris
T +33 1 42 45 46 55

MY FOOD
22 Rue Robespierre, 93100 Montreuil
T +33 1 48 57 99 68

LA MASSARA
70 Rue de Turbigo, 75003 Paris
T +33 1 42 74 13 94
www.la-massara.fr
Mon.-Sun. 12.00-14.30 and 19.15-23.00;
Fri. 12.00-14.30 and 19.15-23.30;
Sat. 12.00-15.00 and 19.15-23.30;
Sun. 12.00-15.00 and 19.15-22.00

LA PULPERIA
11 Rue Richard Lenoir, 75011 Paris
T +33 1 40 09 03 70
www.lapulperiaparis.fr
Thu.-Fri. 12.00-14.30 and 20.00-23.00; Sat. 19.30-23.00

LA TAVERNE DE ZHAO
49 Rue des Vinaigriers, 75010 Paris
T +33 1 40 37 16 21
Thu.-Sun. 12.00-14.30 and 19.00-22.30

L'EPICERIE MUSICALE
55 Bis Quai de Valmy, 75010 Paris
T +33 7 51 65 38 02
www.epiceriemusicale.com
Thu.-Fri. 12.00-15.00 and 18.00-21.00;
Sat.-Sun. 12.00-15.30 and 18.00-21.00

LE 6 PAUL BERT
6 Rue Paul Bert, 75011 Paris
T +33 1 43 79 14 32
Thu. 19.30-23.00; Wed.-Sat. 12.00-14.00 and 19.30-23.00

SERVAN
32 Rue Saint-Maur, 75011 Paris
T +33 1 55 28 51 82
www.leservan.com
Mon. 19.30-22.30; Thu.-Fri. 12.00-14.00 and 19.30-22.30

BOUDOIR

25 Rue du Colisée - 75008 Paris
T +33 1 43 59 25 29 - www.boudoirparis.fr
Mon.-Fri. 12.00-13.30 and 20.00-21.00

I dare say that I am a real lover of sliced cold meat. I don't know approximately how many thousands of kilometres I've detoured knowing that somewhere there is someone who makes a fantastic pâté, a divine sausage or an insanely delicious terrine.

Pâté in a crust of fowl and goose liver

I also have no idea how many kilometres of sausage and how many kilos of wonderful pâté I have consumed so far in my life.

This hidden treasure, situated only a few steps away from the ever busy and popular Champs Elysées, is totally devoted to one of the greatest French forms of art – *the charcuterie.*

The restaurant doesn't really look like a ladies boudoir, but the guests couldn't care less. Arnaud Nicolas, a recipient of the coveted *Meilleur Ouvrier de France* in charcuterie, is in control here. His concept is both special and unique.

In recent times, charcuterie has been subjected to much criticism, which Arnaud thinks is a pity. The media makes no distinction between inferior industrial products, which I wouldn't even feed my pets, and artisanal products made by chefs who know what they're doing. Moreover, charcuterie is not that popular among women who enjoy gourmet food because it usually contains a high fat content.

Therefore, Arnaud and his culinary team are on a mission: they are examining how to reinvent terrines and pâtés as sexy products with far less fat, but without losing their taste and savouriness. They have been busy for a long time with this task and momentarily they have quite a number of recipes that meet these conditions. Charcuterie is an area of gastronomy that usually sees very little innovation. But once you've taken a tour of this place, you'll think differently.

The dishes look very modern and every one of them is finger-licking good. The *pâté en croûte de volaille et foie gras* does not contain one gram of redundant fat which is amazing, because even a fervent pâté eater like myself has not noticed it. Then comes the magical moment, just like the tension a conductor creates in the nano-second of silence before the first notes of Beethoven's 5th Symphony. That magical moment is cutting a slice of pâté and bringing it to your mouth. The first bite will be enough to convince you that charcuterie is a very serious business in this place. The pâté makes you sit still and be totally affected by it. Everything is perfect, the texture, the wonderfully rough structure, the very complex yet perfect seasoning. You think you're dreaming.

The dishes are small pieces of art that look like they're made for charcuterie. And that is exactly the ambition of this establishment. Top charcuterie disguised as gastronomic dishes. And Boudoir does this wonderfully well.

CHEZ AKRAME

19 Rue Lauriston - 75016 Paris
T +33 1 40 67 11 16 - www.akrame.com
Mon.-Fri. 12.00-13.30 and 20.00-21.30

In 2004, Benallal Akrame took a plunge and mailed his spontaneous candidacy to Ferran Adrià.
He was accepted and learned a great deal, not necessarily about cooking,
but mainly about philosophy.

Green
on
green

Akrame spent the first thirteen years of his life in Algeria and the aromas and impressions of his childhood still inspire his superb and spontaneous kitchen. His cooking is very emotional, which fits perfectly with his flamboyant character. His mother was a fantastic cook and from her he learned the secret of the kitchen that distinguishes between a big dish and a good dish: love! Akrame is a man of perseverance, someone who knows what he wants and where he wants to go. The 25 km between his home and his first apprenticeship job, a restaurant in Molineu, he managed to cover every day by hitchhiking.

In the charming Rue Lauriston, he found empty premises that used to be a bistro of Guy Savoy. He felt immediately at home in the place with its lovely daylight and began to lash out his talent on the Parisians. "All that matters is work,"

say Andy Warhol and I think this motto is tattooed on Akrames' heart. After all, this man has no fear of work; super-hard work is about all he has done since arriving in France at the age of fourteen.

Even at his level, there is still plenty of room in the kitchen for improvisation, for creating dishes à la minute and for spontaneity. That is a rare gift, which not too many chefs possess. A meal prepared by this charismatic chef is like a journey, through the market, via his dreams, past his mother's kitchen, into the depth of his soul. Indeed, it you really observe and taste his dish, you will find yourself looking deep into Akrame's soul. And there are not that many chefs who can let you into their soul. Moreover, Akrame presents his creativity and finesse in a modern style, naturally, without forgetting the know-how he acquired from his masters. A rare talent to be cherished.

ÉTUDE

14 Rue du Bouquet de Longchamp - 75116 Paris
T +33 1 45 05 11 41 - www.etudeparis.fr
Thu.-Fri. 12.30-14.00 and 20.00-22.00; Sat. 20.00-22.00

You would never stumble upon this restaurant by accident while wandering about Paris. This gem is hidden on the lovely Rue du Bouquet de Longchamp and it is a very conscientiously chosen place for discreet business under the radar.

Imperial Ossetra Caviar Croquette

I have yet to come across a more intimate and relaxing restaurant. Everything here evokes tranquillity and harmony.

The young Japanese chef, Yamagishi Keisuke, has everything under control. He greatly appreciates classical music, especially Chopin's *Études* (solo pieces for piano), which is where the name of the restaurant comes from. He shares his passion via the kitchen and creates what he calls an evolutionary cuisine. His always studies his dishes carefully and then subtly adjusts them. In the end, every detail counts and makes a difference.

Yamagishi comes from Nagano and became totally enamoured with the classical French cuisine in Osawa, Tokyo. His dream was to give his own interpretation to his cherished cuisine in Paris, and that's just what he has done!

You are given a menu that consists of snapshots of dishes. The menu is actually an entirety and it rises in crescendo, like a piece of classical music. This also occurs in the dining room. When you enter this small and lovely restaurant, you right away notice the austere way in which the tables are set:

only a napkin and a water glass. At the end of the meal, the tables are returned to this condition.

The dishes are totally refined, an exercise in composition, texture, colour and taste. By experimenting with various temperatures, it seems as if temperature is used almost like seasoning.

This pure, enigmatic, seasonally-oriented cuisine is galvanised by carefully selected suppliers. For example, all the vegetables are supplied by the iconic Joel Thibault. Also the wine list shows evidence of in-depth research for pure wines with obvious class. Burgundy wines in particular are well represented here.

Although the caviar croquette appears to be the epitome of decadence, it is actually a very modest, yet deep and proper dish that optimally expresses the taste of caviar. The bite and temperature provide just the right frame for giving the caviar its main role. There are very few chefs who can efface themselves and let their creations do the talking by providing them with the proper carriers.

This exceptionally talented chef is waiting to be discovered.

LA MAISON DE L'AUBRAC

NON·STOP
SERVICE
7/7
Organic
Steack
House
Aligot
WINE

LA MAISON DE L'AUBRAC

37 Rue Marbeuf - 75008 Paris
T +33 1 43 59 05 14 - www.maison-aubrac.com
Sun.-Tue. 12.00-01.00, Wed.-Sat. 12.00-06.00

The Valette family in Laguiole have been breeding Aubrac cattle for three generations. Christian Valette, who was born in Paris where his parents had met, is a jack-of-all-trades; on the one hand, a man of the fields and on the other, a more than successful restaurant owner in Paris.

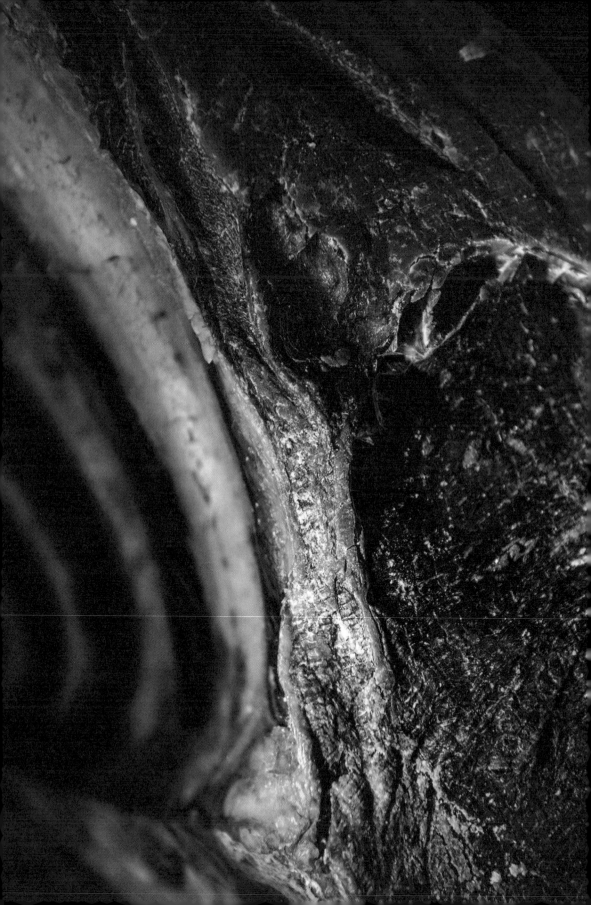

Rib steak

After completing his studies in cooking and agriculture, he took over Le Petit Berry on Rue Marbeuf from his parents. His idea of offering samples of quality products from the Aubrac region had an immediate and strong effect. Since then – from 1998 – he has been commuting between Paris and the Aubrac region. In the area of quality beef, he is definitely a visionary.

His family business, La Ferme des Vialars, is a model business by all standards. Two herds of Aubrac cattle graze on the high plateaus. They enjoy abundant space and their welfare is closely monitored. Their diet consists of cereals and vegetables planned by a food specialist to meet the strictest of quality standards.

Therefore, Valette has every reason to be proud of his Aubrac: the meat cuts in his restaurant are displayed like jewels under lock and key! Two to eighteen cows are slaughtered each week for the restaurant, in the busier weeks up to 22.

Maison de l'Aubrac is the place for anyone who wants to eat a wonderful and healthy cut of beef. Everything here is related to beef and since the recent renovations, the place offers more insight and transparency into the production. After all, customers here automatically become more articulate and demanding when it comes to food quality.

Laurent Durot, the principal chef, is simply indulging and offers a traditional range of beef dishes (such as French beef stew, carpaccio, tartare) and of course the beyond-fantastic grilled and broiled cuts of Aubrac beef, with or without *aligot* (cheese blended into mashed potatoes).

La Maison de l'Aubrac is the type of place where you run into everyone you know, because beef, after all, is one of the greatest French culinary treasures which apparently everyone loves. Combine this with one of the best wine lists in the French capital and you've found a place you will always want to go back to.

LA TABLE DE LANCASTER

7 Rue de Berri - 75008 Paris
T +33 1 40 76 40 18 - www.latabledulancaster.fr
Mon-Fri. 12.30-14.00 and 19.30-22.00

You're only a stone's throw away from the ever busy Champs Elysées,
yet it seems as if you have landed on a different planet.

Royal crayfish decorated with shiso, on a bed of Ossetra caviar consommé

The unobtrusive, yet gorgeous, Lancaster Hotel conceals one of the best-kept top establishments in Paris: La Table de Lancaster.

The decor seems immune to the trends that blow through Paris, because this place emanates delightful timelessness that makes you feel very much at ease, in spite of the delicate luxury that it commands.

Most of the top tables in Paris are subjected to excessive media attention and many chefs push and shove to appear on the next idiotic television show. However, there are also chefs who carve their own path at their own tempo and in full discretion.

Julien Roucheteau is such a personality. He started at the grill in La Maison de l'Aubrac, moved to Le Cinq and is now the chef at La Table de Lancaster. All this occurred in a radius of a few hundred metres. In La Table de Lancaster, he first worked under chef Michel Troisgros, who in 2008 offered him the position of chef.

Roucheteau is a proponent of contemporary *'cuisine bourgeoise'* (bourgeois or plain cooking), which is totally wrapped around the tradition of the French haute cuisine. His dishes are subtle, refined and immensely tasty. He succeeds in creating a very personal kitchen with high-quality products and basic ingredients. You feel his tremendous mastery: he is unchallenged in the way he manages flavours and textures.

Obviously, everyone is welcome here. After all, it is a restaurant, but the type you want to cherish and share only with your best friends. This dream restaurant should really remain a secret so that the bucolic tranquillity that reins here will always allow us to drift off to our culinary dream world.

LE CLARENCE À L'HÔTEL DILLON

31 Avenue Franklin Roosevelt - 75008 Paris
T +33 1 82 82 10 10 - www.le-clarence.paris
Thu.-Sat. 12.30-14.00 and 19.30-21.30

It is not often that a newly opened restaurant becomes an immediate craze and radiates as much class and experience as Le Clarence. The prestigious owners of Château Haut-Brion, La Mission Haut-Brion and Château Quintus opened Le Clarence at the end of 2015 in their 18th century hotel, le Dillon.

Menu C
Éphémère

The restaurant is named after the man who bought Haut-Brion in 1935. The building, today known as Hôtel Dillon, was built in 1884 ironically very close to the place where Château Haut- Brion was named Premier Grand Cru Classé du Médoc in 1855 at the International Exposition in Paris.

The mission of this illustrious family to have a top restaurant goes far back in history.

At the coronation of Henry II in 1660, Haut-Brion was served and in 1666 François-Auguste de Pontac, direct ancestor of Clarence Dillon, opened the Pontack's Head in London of those early years. Everyone came to this chic French tavern to savour the newest Claret and rich and fashionable people passed through here.

In 1801, Charles-Maurice de Talley-rand, former minister of foreign affairs under Napoleon, bought Haut-Brion. He used the super elegant wines of Haut-Brion as a diplomatic and politi-cal weapon and as a means of leverage. Many members of royalty around the world came to his restaurant to dine and drink his wines and of course to taste the culinary masterpieces of a certain Antonin Carême, one of the greatest chefs ever. Thomas Jefferson was the best imaginable ambassador for Haut-Brion and to this day the wine is regularly served at the White House.

Even before Clarence Dillon invested in this top Bordeaux domain, he already owned shares in haute gas-tronomy particularly in Plaza Athénée and Taillevent, which as a result of his input developed into to what they are today. The history of Haut-Brion is inextricably connected with elegant gastronomy, so a top restaurant is the logical consequence.

The primary choice for a chef at the cooking range was Christophe Pelé, who several years ago surprised friends and foes when he gave up his 2-star La Bigarrade and embarked on a journey. The choice for the dining room was Antoine Petrus, one of the best sommeliers. Their talents combine here to create pure magic in the form of gigantic bouquets reminiscent of a 19th century painting.

Here you find yourself in a large house abundant with obvious class: thick car-pets, beautiful Christofle silverware, a library collected by Déborah Dupont of the Librairie Gourmande, and delicate porcelain from Nymphenburg. The shadow of the Grand Palace looms between the branches of ancient oak trees. Here you are in a top restaurant, managed by the best staff you'll ever find, full of devotion and knowledge.

Cooking goes beyond following a rec-ipe, and receiving guests is an art form. Here you experience this first-hand.

LE FRANK

À la Fondation Louis Vuitton - 8 Avenue du Mahatma Gandhi - 75116 Paris
T +33 1 58 44 25 70 - www.restaurantlefrank.fr
Mon., Wed. & Thu. 12.00-19.00, dinner with reservation; Fri. 11.00-23.00; Sat.-Sun. 11.00-20.00

Le Frank must be one of the few restaurants in the world named after an architect.
And the master builder is not just any architect: Frank Gehry is a phenomenon.

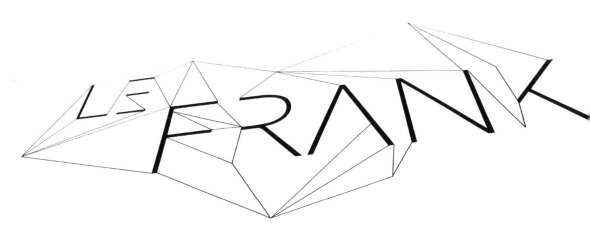

Lemon pie

He has permanently changed the way we look at architecture. His monumental works shine all over the world. No one can remain indifferent about his Guggenheim Museum in Bilbao. Paris has honoured him with the Fondation Louis Vuitton; an impressive building. It's only regrettable that the letters LV at the front of the building are too obtrusive and attract too much attention. The commercial overstatement is clearly a false note in this beautiful and serene building. But as soon as you get past that moment – with me it takes perhaps a bit longer – you will rediscover the expected elegance of Louis Vuitton.

I am glad that the museum restaurants have reinstated their honour. I think nothing is more frustrating than visiting a beautiful museum – experiencing total quality – and then having to make do with a prefab sandwich that I would not serve to my worst enemy. Fortunately, there is currently a refresher movement in motion. Take, for example, 't Zilte in Antwerp, The Modern in New York City or this Le Frank in Paris.

Jean-Louis Nomicos was hired by Fondation Louis Vuitton to prepare dishes that are worthy of this building. Nomi-

cos, a chef with a history of employment in Michelin star restaurants, was ready for this serious challenge. A museum restaurant of course has a different beat than the normal lunch-dinner frequency of other restaurants. A huge challenge for a chef of his calibre. He has certainly passed the test with flying colours! You can come here for breakfast, for lunch, and on Friday and Saturday evenings, for dinner.

The leitmotif is a very natural cuisine, tasty and scented, reasonably loyal to the traditional French cuisine but with just a hint of the exotic. Nomicos takes both small and big eaters into account: both children and adults. The afternoon is characterised by small dishes and desserts, whereupon Nomicos shows his obvious class with a well-made lemon meringue pie, my all-time favourite. The kitchen's tempo is adapted to the visitor.

Le Frank is a fantastic place in an amazingly beautiful building in the middle of a forest. Cooking here is a privilege for any chef. Nomicos steps back and lets the simplicity of his dishes do the talking, and in the shadow of Frank Gehry, that is the best that a chef can do.

LE PRÉ CATELAN

Bois de Boulogne - Route de Suresnes - 75000 Paris
T +33 1 44 14 41 14 - www.restaurant.leprecatelan.com
Thu.-Sat. 12.00-13.30 and 19.30-21.30

Le Pré Catelan is an impressive restaurant from every perspective. It is one of those places
that one enters humbly and with great respect. This entire establishment emanates history and
decadence, but at a very human level.

Menu du Pré

The history of Le Pré Catelan began in 1905 on the drawing board of the architect, Guillaume Tronchet, who was commissioned by the City of Paris to build a luxury casino/restaurant at this unique site in the Bois de Boulogne.

The city gave the concession to the owner of Chez Paillard on the Champs Elysées. In 1908, Léopold Mourier, owner of the world-famous Fouquet's, took over the restaurant part of Le Pré Catelan, which at that time had become the city's hotspot.

Le Pré Catelan reached its culinary peak in 1923 when Charles Drouant, who already owned a very lovely restaurant on Place Gaillon, took over the entire establishment after Mourier passed away and elevated Le Pré Catelan to an unparalleled level.

In 1976, the current owners, Colette and Gaston Lenôtre, entered the business and renovated the restaurant in an impressive style.

The super talent of Frédéric Anton is very quickly recognised by all the chefs who have worked with him. Since the start of his career in 1984, Anton has worked alongside many great chefs including Gérard Veissière, Robert Bardot and later Gérard Boyer and Joël Robuchon. In 1997, he accepted Lenôtre's offer to become the chef of Le Pré Catelan, a job that he fulfils with passion.

The kitchen is flooded with natural light and this is apparently very inspiring. Just like the guest dining room, it is almost completely part of the beautiful décor of Bois de Boulogne. There is no place for imperfection in Anton's kitchen. Precision, balance and generosity have become the trademarks of this dream restaurant that should be on everyone's bucket list. At every level you will find the kind of grandeur that made Paris famous. The impeccable service, perfect dishes and superb cellar create a dream environment in which everything is absolutely awesome. It can't possibly get better.

OKUDA

Rue de la Tremoille - 75008 Paris
T +33 1 40 70 19 19 - www.okuda.fr
Wed.-Sat. 12.00-13.30 and 18.30-21.30

A Japanese enclave in Paris. I often travel to Japan and there are very few places around the world – outside of Japan – where I have experienced an authentic sense of Japan. Stepping into Okuda is truly like entering Japan. Toru Okuda, a *kaiseki* grand master has two top restaurants in Ginza, one of the most beautiful districts in the Japanese capital. His restaurants have two and three Michelin stars, respectively.

Kaiseki

When he was eighteen, Okuda was hired as a chauffeur and shoe polisher in a culinary inn in his native city of Shizuoka, along the coast. He had never touched a kitchen knife before, yet slowly but surely he became absolutely enamoured by the Japanese kitchen. He dug his heels into this world, as only the Japanese know how to do. At the expense of his sleep, he devoured everything ever written about *kaiseki*, the highest Japanese culinary art, and practiced cutting techniques. He began working in the kitchen and it soon became clear that he had exceptional talent. He participated in very stringent apprenticeships supervised by the most rigorous masters in Kyoto and Tokushima. In 1999, Okuda opened his first virtuoso *kaiseki* restaurant in his native city of Shizuoka and became one of the youngest, respected *kaiseki* masters with exceptional skills and an aptitude for harmony and composition. He created a more explicit version of the great Japanese classics without superfluous luxury and seasoning – just pure perfection.

"First we take Manhattan, then we take Berlin" is what Okuda must have thought when he opened his first restaurant Ginza Kojyu in the very mundane Ginza district. It was immediately awarded three stars in the first Michelin Tokyo. His second restaurant, Ginza Okuda, in the same neighbourhood, immediately received two Michelin stars when it opened in 2011.

Okuda has the greatest respect for the French culinary grand masters. He saw them all come to Japan for inspiration and in order to allow the Japanese to enjoy the top French kitchens. By now, Robuchon, Ducasse, Bocuse and Troisgros have outposts in Tokyo. The Japanese kitchen is very dear to Okuda and he maintains that it's very difficult to find a reliable Japanese kitchen outside of Japan; I agree completely with that. Okuda focussed on Paris, which for him is the capital of taste. In Paris, he opened a genuine piece of Japan, with an eye for detail that I have yet to see outside of Japan.

Here he has introduced the authentic Japanese kitchen, and not one adapted for Western palates, but simply as it is. For this purpose, he imports many condiments and products that he also uses in his restaurants in Japan. Whereas in the French haute cuisine one adds flavours in order to achieve a better entirety, *kaiseki* is more about austerity and eliminating seasoning in order to reach the essence of a top product.

The total experience of a *kaiseki* menu is a moment of *mono no aware, Weltschmerz, lacrimae rerum, saudade* or whatever you want to call it. It is a ritual, a superb moment of contemplation and consecration, a moment of humility for so much intensity and beauty. Yet to fully enjoy this beauty, it must be destroyed; after all we have to eat it. The ultimate way of communicating without words that can be compared with a musical piece in which the composer provides the tempo, rhythm and intensity.

The *kizuna* – the bond – between me and this restaurant is very strong. This restaurant should be on everyone's bucket list.

PIERRE GAGNAIRE

6 Rue Balzac - 75008 Paris
T +33 1 58 36 12 50 - www.pierre-gagnaire.com
Mon.-Fri. 12.30-13.30 and 19.30-21.30

When I sat at a table for the first time at Pierre Gagnaire, which was then located in St-Etienne, I was incredibly impressed. Awed by the architectural masterpiece of a building and impressed mainly by the carefreeness with which Pierre Gagnaire poopooed the various conventions.

Menu Esprit Pierre Gagnaire

Top dishes served on smashed pieces of windowpane were the epitome of non-convention. Gagnaire has of course developed into the iconic chef of his generation, especially as a front man for the fusion cuisine movement in haute gastronomy. From the start of his career, he has nibbled at the conventions of the classic French art of cooking and experimented with contrasting combinations in taste, texture and ingredients. He sees himself as someone who is facing the future with respect for the past.

Gagnaire is fascinated by painters, because they use their talents to say things that cannot be said in other circumstances. Whether he wants to or not, a painter uses his canvas to share his emotions and visions with the rest of the world. Gagnaire wants to create the same poetry on his plates. He is one of the first chefs to perceive a chef as an artist and he dates his dishes like painters date their artworks.

His kitchen is about the chef's unpretentiousness and the unpretentiousness of the person who will taste the dish. Gagnaire finds this field of tension fascinating. Yet, just like every modern artist, Gagnaire has a solid classical base. He worked at Bocuse and at Senderens before he took over his father's starred restaurant, le Clos Fleuri in St-Etienne.

Gagnaire works occasionally with the renowned French chemist, Hervé This, the father of molecular gastronomy who works for the National Institute of Agricultural Research at AgroParisTech, researching the chemical processes behind cooking techniques that at times are very simple. This shares Gagnaire's affection for kitchens and their collaboration enables Gagnaire to explore playfully certain taste combinations and cooking techniques.

It was made clear that France was not ready for Gagnaire's eccentric dishes by the fact that his business in St-Etienne went bankrupt in the mid 1990s. With the help of a few friends, he was able to re-start in Paris in 1996. Two years later, he managed to recover his three Michelin stars.

A meal at Gagnaire is like a walk through an exhibition; it is a story that he began to tell a long time ago. His kitchen is based on honesty and intuition, and his ability to combine tastes that at first sight seem most unlikely is a sixth sense.

An evening at Gagnaire is an adventure, full of surprises and above all, unforgettable.

SCHWARTZ'S DELI

22 Avenue Niel - 75017 Paris
T +33 1 42 67 65 79 - www.schwartzsdeli.fr
Mon.-Fri. 12.00-15.00 and 19.30-23.00; Sat. 12.00-17.00 and 19.00-23.30; Sun. 12.00-17.00 and 19.00-23.00

Pastrami is a little like a journey in time. It is an age-old method of preserving meat
by pickling it, drying it slightly, mixing it with various herbs and afterwards
slowly smoking it and steaming it.

Pastrami sandwich

Pastrami is a little like a journey in time

According to lore, its origins are not entirely clear. It might have originated in Turkey where it is called *pastirma* and perhaps in Romania where *pastra* means as much as 'to store'. We will never be sure. What is for certain is that the first *pastrami* sandwiches in NY emerged during the wave of Rumanian-Jewish immigration from Romania and Bessarabia. In Yiddish it was called *pastrome*, which evolved into *pastrama* in English and later, analogous to salami, it became pastrami.

Sussman Volk, a kosher butcher, received a pastrami recipe from a Romanian friend and made the first pastrami sandwich in 1887. This became so popular that his butcher's shop had to make way for a restaurant, which became the iconic Katz's delicatessen on the Lower East Side of Manhattan. In my opinion, they turned the pastrami sandwich into the popular item that it is today. The people who opened Schwartz's Deli were inspired by the Katz bastion and did their level best to give their coleslaw the right NYC feel.

Although the pastrami here is made from veal, it is still one of the best versions that I have eaten – except for Katz's pastrami sandwich. The chips are nice and light and the pastrami is piled high enough to make you homesick for North America very quickly; and rightfully so. There are currently three Schwartz's in Paris, but the flagship is on Rue des Écouffes, which I call the Jewish Street. The wonderful thing about this place is that Katz's is a real deli. It is so lovely that it has been taken over by hipsters, and for an evening bite you really need to make a reservation. I must admit that if you squint your eyes enough, you'll think you're on East Houston...

Reserve a table in a deli? That's new for me.

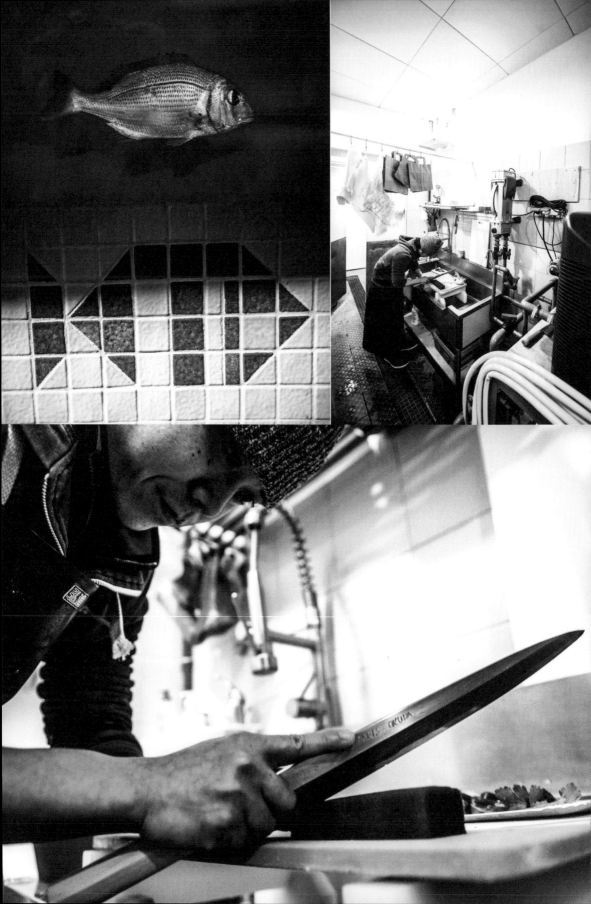

SHINICHI

35 Rue Duret - 75116 Paris
T +33 1 44 17 93 58
Mon. 09.00-15.00; Tue.-Fri. 09.00-13.00 and 15.00-20.00; Sat. 09.00-20.00

What in heaven's name is wrong with me? Even when I'm at the zoo, strolling around the aquarium with my children, it hits me. While everyone gazes at a beautiful and mysterious fish, I can only think of the incredible sashimi that could probably be made from that particular fish. I can almost see *sashimi* portions swimming around the water.

 ㈱伊東活魚
(f)(S.A) ITO-KATUGYO
JAPAN 0557 (37) 6988

Sashimi special

That's why I had a déjà vu in this *saka-naya,* a typical Japanese fishmonger store located just a few steps from Porte Maillot.

I think I can safely assume that by now anyone who knows something about food will agree with me that Japan is pre-eminently the country for preparing fish. A fishmonger's store is a sort of holy shrine. And a store with a nice selection of live fish, where you can get your *sashimi* every day or eat on location, is the holy of holies. The concept is simple, yet complex, due to an uncompromising fish-killing technique that preserves the quality of the fish meat.

Top fish species are usually supplied live to this store by small line-fishermen and the fish are kept alive in large Japanese pools until their fate is determined. Fish are not suffocated but are killed using ikejime, an almost ritual slaughter and age-long technique which is totally in contrast to our means of killing fish. The purpose is to limit the formation of lactic acid in the muscle tissue and thereby keeping the fish meat fresh and firm for longer. First of all, the fish maw, which is found

behind the gills, is emptied by pricking it with a needle. Afterwards, the fish is placed in a receptacle with seawater to relax it so that any lactic acid formed in the muscles during the catch can be eliminated. After a while, the live fish is placed on a cutting board and a type of thick needle is inserted in the brain. The reaction is immediate; the fins stretch and 'freeze', the mouth falls open and the fish stiffens as if paralysed. Subsequently, via the gills, the small area in between the vertebrae is cut through so that the fish bleeds to death. Thus, no suffocation and no lactic acid as there is in our method. Subsequently, a few centimetres are cut off at the tail end, providing an easy start for threading a flexible iron thread through the spine up to the brain. The fish, including the intestines, is then placed in ice-cold water to bleed out.

The quality of the fish meat using *ikejime* is astoundingly better than when using our method. Skilled hands and knives cut these fish in this mini *Tsukiji* market where unbelievable high quality is the standard and nothing less! A must for any lover of sashimi, and aren't we all that, even if just a bit?

SUSHI OKUDA

18 Rue du Boccador - 75008 Paris
T +33 1 47 20 17 18 - www.sushiokuda.com
Wed.-Sat. 12.00-13.30 and 18.30-22.00

"My life will never be the same," said a good friend of mine when he took a bite of a sea urchin
sushi (*uni:* Japanese for edible part of the sea urchin) for the first time in a top sushi bar.
I had warned him nonetheless.

Sushi

He had already swum through many Japanese food-serving watering holes, but he had never had the opportunity to eat real sushi worthy of being called Japanese.

Many people don't believe or cannot possibly imagine that it takes 10-15 years to perfect the skill of making sushi. Sushi's long history has evolved over time, and this needs to be evident in the taste. Anyone in Japan who wants to be taken seriously as a sous chef, must devote years to this goal and only the best ever reach the status of *shokunin*. I have rarely tasted this perfection outside of Japan, but here in Okuda it's unmistakable.

Eating sushi should be a complete sensory experience. Everything must be perfect. Stepping into this restaurant provides temporary release from the pressures of this worldly city. Although the restaurant is located only a few hundred metres from the chaotic commotion of L'Etoile, you feel as if you have entered a bubble. You are in a Japanese cocoon; a necessary condition, like the silence before a beautiful musical piece.

The establishment is always full, yet no one is stressed. These sushi chefs become one with their work, they become a true medium of the product, the catalysts for transforming rice and fish into a magical tasting experience. They possess ultimate focus, a quality that apparently only Japanese have.

A perfect sushi tastes better than its individual ingredients; only Japanese products are used and the fish is pure pedigree caught by the best fishermen. Every sushi is an adventure, a mini tasting menu in one bite. It begins with the feather-light rice. It looks like a fluffy cloud, which makes people wonder how the grains manage to stick to each other. The temperature of the entire meal is always lukewarm.

Once you're sitting comfortably at this restaurant decorated completed in *hinoki* (Japanese cypress) – which must have cost a fortune – Tokyo is only a stone's throw away. This is all part of the total experience. The choice for market-fresh, skilfully handled fish is astounding; the only stress factor is deciding what to order. As it should be, *nigiri,* is sensibly prepared to reach an explicit taste, as you would expect in a top sushi bar in Tokyo.

Sushi Okuda is probably the best sushi bar on the European continent.

TORAYA

10 Rue Saint-Florentin - 75001 Paris
T +33 1 42 60 13 00 - www.toraya-group.co.jp/toraya-paris
Mon.-Sat. 10.30-19.00

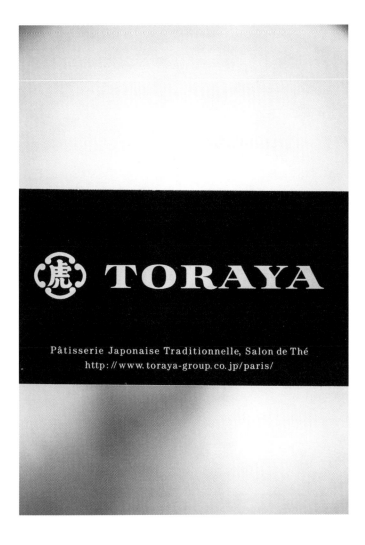

The Japanese kitchen and the Japanese influences on the highest echelons of our Western culinary culture have never been as strong as they are today. Yet, there is at least one aspect of the ingenious and subtle Japanese kitchen that somehow has not really penetrated the Western culinary scene, namely the *wagashi*, the mysterious art of preparing petite and very refined sweets.

Wagashi — petite and very refined sweets

Wagashi is a traditional Japanese confectionery, where is usually served with tea. Neither milk nor eggs are ever used; the most common basic ingredients are *anko* (pasta made from adzuki beans), *igname, wasanbonto*, rice and fruit.

Making sweet dishes by adding unrefined sugar was never a Japanese tradition in the old days and this is made clear by the traditional word for sweetness, *okashi,* which always refers to nuts and fruit. It took until the Muromachi period (1337-1573), with the growing popularity of visiting traditional tea-houses and the emergence of dim sum, that some wise men and philosophers brought wagashi from China. I actually prefer to call wagashi sweet dim sum. This rich cultural period in Japanese history during which the beautiful gold *kinkaku-ji* temple in Kyoto was built (among other highlights) is also characterised by the international rise of trade relationships with Japan.

Although the Portuguese traded regularly from 1543, the Spaniards from 1587 and the Dutch from 1609, the Japanese sweets at that time were not to the taste of Western traders, who nonetheless identified trading opportunities almost everywhere else they looked.

The noble art of wagashi finally flourished in Japan during the following period, known as the Edo Period (24 March 1603-3 May 1868). This period, under the rule of one of the most iconic shoguns, Tokugawa Ieyasu, brought great stability and peace to Japan, allowing the high culture to blossom.

Wagashi comes in all scents and colours, but it is always based on the seasons. I mostly look forward to the arrival of the chestnut season, a very tasty nut in Japan. Within the product range of a big factory such as Minamoto Kitchoan, there is naturally a place for season-based products. I'm always determined to visit this place for the *oribenishiki* and *kurishigure*, two creations that bring out the best in chestnuts. Just like in many Japanese recipes, the chief ingredient is the most significant one. Here the chestnut is purified, sugared or processed in some other way and a bit of unrefined sugar, such as *wasanbon,* and rice are added for the texture. Nothing more is needed to be blown away by the power of simplicity.

Wagashi always looks lovely, a paragon of aesthetic perfection as is only innate to the Japanese.

All this suddenly becomes clear when you stand in front of the shop window of Toraya, established approximately 30 years ago in Paris. No overkill of whipped cream cakes, but an exercise in Zen that reflects the seasons. As soon as you step in, it becomes even clearer: an oasis of tranquillity where the sound of a Japanese bamboo flute prevails and the waiters seem to float across the floor. The tradition and tranquillity that reigns here are monumental. Mitsuhiro Kurokawa is the 17th generation head of this traditional house in Kyoto. This house was established in 1520 and has been supplying the royal court of Japan since the middle of the 16th century. *Tora,* which means tiger, clearly explains the emblem of the house. A visit to Toraya is truly an invitation to poetry...

ADDITIONAL EATERIES

PLACE DE L'ÉTOILE / CHAMPS ÉLYSÉES / PLACE DE LA CONCORDE

BŒUF SUR LE TOIT
34 Rue du Colisée, 75008 Paris
T +33 1 53 93 65 55
www.boeufsurletoit.com
Mon.-Sun. 12.00-15.00 and 19.00-23.00

L'ATELIER DE ROBUCHON ÉTOILE
Publicis Drugstore
133 Av. des Champs-Élysées, 75008 Paris
T +33 1 47 23 75 75
www.publicisdrugstore.com
Mon.-Sun. 11.30-15.30 and 18.30-00.00

ATSUSHI TANAKA

4 Rue du Cardinal Lemoine - 75005 Paris
T +33 1 56 81 94 08 - www.atsushitanaka.com
Thu.-Sat. 12.15-14.00 and 20.00-21.30

One tends to associate Rue du Cardinal Lemoine with a classic culinary centre; after all, the world-famous La Tour d'Argent restaurant is right around the corner.

Camouflage

Nowadays however, many lovers of gourmet cuisine walk past it and cross to the other side of the street to the modest little restaurant of the ultra-cool Japanese chef, Atsushi Tanaka.

Atsushi does not cook Japanese style and certainly not French. He is one of those chefs who from a young age learned how to develop his own unique form, which is a rare and welcomed quality in an era of rampant culinary plagiarism. His track record is nothing less than fabulous. Atsushi has worked at Quique Dacosta, Bart de Pooter, Sergio Herman and has trained at Geranium, Frantzén and Oaxen Krog. Master chef Pierre Gagnaire viewed the young Atsushi as his new muse and already on his 18th birthday he crowned him "Picasso of the Kitchen". This was no small compliment and it placed a heavy weight on the shoulders of this young man, who refers to his mentor as 'Papa'.

As a result of this experience, but mainly due to his inquisitiveness, Atsushi developed his dynamic, modern, progressive and artistic cuisine, which cannot be pigeonholed because of his very personal interpretations of the various influences that he has experienced. His dishes have a very high sense of composition and they are nothing less than breathtakingly beautiful. But of course, that's only the start: the tastes are just right and that's why this small and simple establishment is tipped by the world press as one of the most exciting new restaurants.

Nevertheless, when the restaurant opened in April 2014, most French journalists thought Atsushi was just another run-of-the-mill Japanese chef who cooked French cuisine. That quickly turned out to be a far too superficial analysis and Atsushi says himself that just because he was born in Japan doesn't make him a Japanese chef.

Atsushi opts for balance, both in flavours and in ingredients. His youth in Japan has led to valuable reflection in this area: the key to this balance is in controlling the strong flavours, combined with delicate ingredients. For example, this is why he never uses soya sauce, even though this ingredient would be so natural for someone of his origin.

I think he is a wonderful and fascinating raconteur when he relates his culinary travels, interspersed with flashbacks of his youth. Certain things he leaves open so that the listener can fill in and dream away.

A superstar in the making...

207

SAINT-GERMAIN-DES-PRÉS / MONTPARNASSE / JARDIN DES PLANTES

CLOVER

5 Rue Perronet - 75007 Paris
T +33 1 75 50 00 05 - www.clover-paris.com
Tue.-Sat. 12.30-14.00 and 19.30-22.00

There are only twenty seating places in this jewel of a restaurant, which appears to attract mainly people from the fashion world.

Cuisine of the day

The restaurant is so small that everything becomes part of the décor, including the elongated kitchen.

In 2009, top-notch and smart chef Jean-François Piège left Le Crillon – after receiving his second star – to start building his own imperium on the left bank of the Seine. It all started with the Thoumieux brasserie and hotel and, of course, his Jean-François Piège restaurant with its retro rat-pack decor. By now, he has handed over the baton here too, and recently opened the very beautiful Clover restaurant with his wife Elodie. Piège has always been intrigued by the form of a four-leaf clover and the powers attributed to it. That is why the name is so appropriate.

Clover is fashionable, stylish, yet very cosy and has the atmosphere of a small, intimate club where your favourite jazz singers seem to sing only for you.

Elodie's engaging personality adds human warmth. It is a breath of fresh air to be welcomed by someone who knows what to do rather than someone who stands there waiting to be discovered by a modelling agency.

The kitchen is very instinctive and when you see the cooks busy in their culinary set-up you instantly realise: these are not run-of-the-mill cooks, but the real deal. However, the accent is on lightness, spontaneity and health. It's time for French people to realise that we all eat too much fat and that we have to adapt our diet to our current lifestyle. This is no easy step, because the richness and power of the classic French kitchen is based exactly on those products that Piège tries to eliminate.

I believe that Piège does not need a four-leaf clover to bring luck to his Clover.

LA CUISINE EST L'ART
DE TRANSFORMER
INSTANTANÉMENT
EN JOIE DES PRODUITS
CHARGÉS D'HISTOIRE

GOÛT DE BRIOCHE

54 Rue Mazarine - 75006 Paris
T +33 1 40 46 91 67 - www.goutdebrioche.com
Tue.-Sun. 08.30-19.00

Who doesn't like brioche? A brioche is very versatile because it can be used with both sweet and salty dishes. Moreover, a brioche is undeniably a French invention with a very long history.

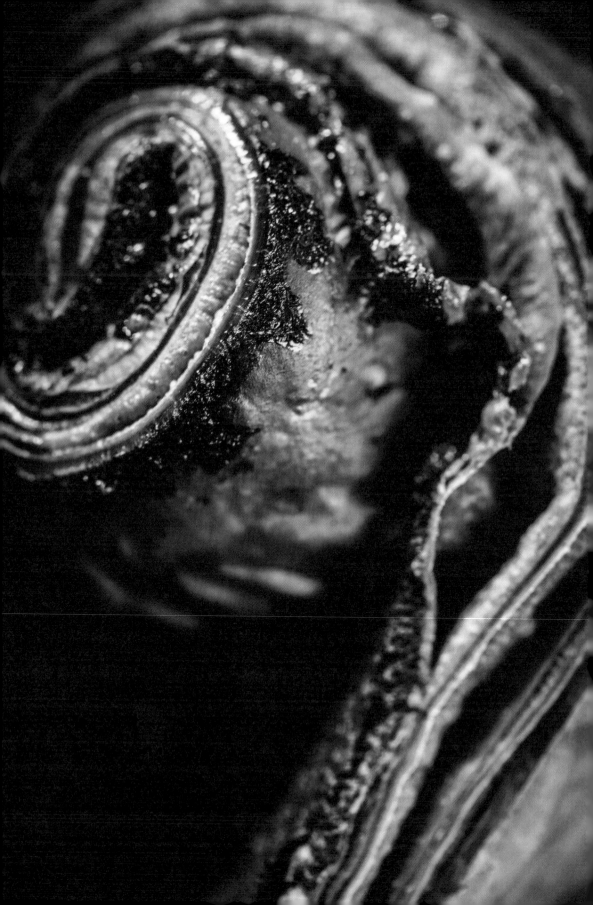

Brioches in all shapes and sizes

The first recorded use of the term brioche was actually in 1404. It also appeared in *A Dictionarie of the French and English Tongues,* compiled by Randle Cotgrave. It belongs to the category of *Viennoiserie* (Danish pastries) and over the years it has evolved from the frugal church baked *pain bénit* (consecrated bread) – that was constantly enriched with increasingly more eggs and butter – until it became the rich *brioche* that we eat nowadays. During the 17th century, the terms *brioche* and *pain bénit* were often used to describe the same product. From the time of Louis XIV, it became clear that the quality and quantity of butter was the secret of a good brioche. That's why the best brioches were baked in markets where the best types of butter were traded. At that time, Gisors was considered one of the best butter markets and on market days sometimes 300 kilos of brioche were baked. What a wonderful scent that must have produced!

Back to Rue Mazarine. Hidden in between art galleries, this lovely boutique restaurant pays tribute to brioche. The proud fathers are Guy Savoy and his pastry chef, Christian Boudard. Top chef Savoy has a special affection for brioche and his signature dish is artichoke soup with truffles and brioche made flaky with mushrooms and truffles. Filled brioche in particular became world famous and that's how the idea was conceived to devote a boutique to brioche in all its forms.

Boudard and Savoy worked to hone the ideal brioche recipe – both sweet and salty. It is actually quite difficult to make a perfect brioche. Technique and handling are of the essence, and if you have a command of both, the result is irresistibly delicious.

As soon as they had the opportunity, the decision was obvious: Goût de Brioche had to be established. Flaky brioche, small or big or very big, sweet or salty, crunchy or smooth, it's darn difficult to choose. You would have to be as tough as nails to walk past this brioche temple and not buy one. Maybe one for the road when you get hungry? But don't kid yourself: once the brioche is in the bag, it won't be long before it's in your mouth!

LA COUPOLE

102 Boulevard du Montparnasse - 75014 Paris
T +33 1 43 20 14 20 - www.lacoupole-paris.com
Mon.-Fri. 08.00-23.00; Sat.-Sun. 08.30-23.00

La Coupole is without a doubt one of the most famous brasseries in Paris. Moreover, it symbolises the history of Montparnasse and the Parisian savoir-vivre in this very special 14th arrondissement, known for two sports that require elbow work: raising glasses and playing *petanque*.

Tatin of endives and scallops

La Coupole is a true art-deco temple, created by two friends from Auvergne, Ernest Fraux and René Lafon. At its grand opening, on the 20th of December 1927, there was a real parade of famous writers, artists and nightlife personalities, and anybody who was anybody from big spenders to beautiful women and obnoxious wives, were all there.

The pillars with their imitation marble patterns and the door with its cubism inspired mosaics appear on the list of historical monuments.

The American bar accommodated the likes of Picasso, Derain, Léger, Man Ray, Soutine and many others as they sat elbow to elbow. Simenon dined here with Josephine Baker, Breton gave De Chirico a cuff on the ear, Matisse drank his beer here and Joyce enjoyed his whisky. Mistinguett received a standing ovation whenever she entered the room, Camus came here to celebrate his Noble Prize and the staff used to fight over who would serve Table 149, Sartre's usual table, because he tipped

generously. Yves Klein wanted to paint one of the pillars in blue, but instead a blue cocktail, which is still on the menu, was conjured up in his honour.

In May 1968, Cohn-Bendit climbed on a table and Patti Smith played guitar, Renaud played his guitar outside for small change and Gainsbourg frequently lunched here on Sundays with Jane Birkin. In 1984, at table 73, Chagall celebrated his birthday and Mitterrand ate his last meal at table 82, a lamb curry.

This lamb curry has been on the menu since 1927, but it has been adapted by the current chef, Vakhtang Meliava. Originally from Île de France, he gave up a career as a pilot in Canada by resolutely choosing the culinary field. He prepares the traditional French kitchen, but in addition he also provides a modern twist to the classic dishes in order to adapt them to the wishes of the modern consumer.

Come and be enchanted by this homage to Parisian life!

LA MOSQUÉE DE PARIS

39 Rue Geoffroy-Saint-Hilaire - 75005 Paris
T +33 1 43 31 14 32
Daily 12.00-15.30 and 19.00-22.30

This is a wonderful place to stop at and enjoy fantastic Middle Eastern food, but for me it's the tea with typical oriental pastries that makes this place a true must-eat. From springtime onwards, the garden is open and the lovely blue mosaics that reflect in the sun give this place a truly unique atmosphere for a city such as Paris.

oriental pastries

You enter a beautiful, large mosque – one of the largest in France – where in addition to a *hamam,* you will find this beautiful restaurant that welcomes everyone all day long.

In 1920, this mosque was founded by Si-Kaddour-Ben Ghabrit, the former chairman of the Institut Musulman in France. He commissioned architects Robert Fournez and Maurice Mantout and hired Moroccan, Algerian and Tunisian craftsmen to properly complete this monumental, traditional building. They worked six years on all the details and the last hand-made cedar wood door was placed in 1926.

The 33-metre minaret towers above the lily-white domes. The entire building is constructed in a harmonious Moors-Spanish style. The architects found much of their inspiration in The Alhambra in Granada.

Tasty mint tea with delicious oriental pastries that look as if they came straight out of One Thousand & One Nights. An unforgettable experience, even if you don't have a sweet tooth.

Because when they're made by people who know what they're doing, these delicacies are really not sickly sweet. On the contrary, what you get is a lovely balance between nuts, honey, dry fruits and dough. Discover *ma'amoul* with dates or with nuts, *makrout, kahb gasal* (little gazelle cones), *kadaïf, bourma* (a variation of baklava), *lokoum* (Turkish Delight) and of course, the world-famous baklava. Baklava was only exported in 1871 from Damascus to Gaziantep, but it was so successful that in 2008 a protected designation of origin was created.

A giant baklava is distinctly different than any other type of baklava due to the large number of paper-thin layers of dough – three centimetres of wonderful sensations – and the use of quality nuts and honey. That makes this baklava an unforgettable sensation. The combination of the crunchy paper-thin dough, the aesthetic aspect and the perfect dose of sweetness is at a three-star level. Spending a leisurely morning here sipping tea and nibbling on fine pastry is a wonderful idea.

L'ATELIER DE JOËL ROBUCHON

5 Rue Montalembert (corner of Rue du Bac) - 75007 Paris
T +33 1 42 22 56 56 - www.atelier-robuchon-saint-germain.com
Daily 11.30-15.30 and 18.30-24.00

One of the first times I nearly fell off my chair out of mere amazement was in the Jamin restaurant where Joël Robuchon was the chef at that time. I was given a choice between the regular menu and the famous truffles menu. When I saw the prices at the bottom of the menu, I knew what I had to choose.

Tasting menu

I knew I should have taken the regular menu but, my heart cried out: Go for the truffles! And that's what I did. During the entire evening, my taste buds were challenged by the most subtle dishes. An unforgettable meal. But to quote the master himself: "There is no such thing as the perfect meal – one can always do better."

Born in Poitiers in 1945, Joël is an exceptionally talented chef. He realised quite early on that his life would be in the kitchen, and when he was fifteen he began to work as a pastry chef in Relais de Poitiers. His intuition told him to join the apprenticeship Compagnon de Tour de France, which gives young people an opportunity to travel and work throughout France. Joël was a fast learner and at the age of 31 he was awarded the prestigious *Meilleur Ouvrier de France* (MOF) in cuisine, and in 1989 he was awarded the Chef of the Century title by the Gault et Millau restaurant guide. In 1981, he opened his first restaurant, Jamin, in the 16th arrondissement of Paris, which already at that time had become known as one of the best restaurants in the world.

Seeing many of his colleagues suffer from health problems, he decided to retire on his 50th birthday in 1995. But he couldn't sit still for long. He made a comeback and opened various restaurants all over the world and became a TV chef on TF1, where he gave the fiercely watched TV programme, *Bon Appétit*, a new image.

His merciless perfectionism became his trademark and he grew into one of the most influential post-war chefs. He was a key figure in reforming the classic French cuisine into a more authentic, bourgeois one, away from the nouvelle cuisine and its extreme reductionism.

He sought his inspiration mainly in simplicity, and by creating a delicate style with immense respect for natural ingredients, each true to its own flavour, he became a beacon for others.

There are two Atelier de Joël Robuchon in the French capital, one at L'Étoile and the other in St-Germain. This very innovative and subtle concept offers a totally open kitchen, which opens on to a bar that meanders through the restaurant that can seat 40 guests. This creates a magical interaction between the guest and his/her personal chef, a unique concept in the world of haute gastronomy. There are many options here, and everything is negotiable. There is enormous flexibility vis-à-vis the guest. Even great classics can be ordered in tasting portions.

Pierre-Yves Rochon designed the extraordinary interior, which radiates both class and refined conviviality, and the executive chef is Axel Manes.

In a brief period of time, Atelier de Robuchon has grown into an inescapable establishment, a must-do. This freemason has seen his restaurants turn into renowned places of worldwide pilgrimage and he currently holds no less than 25 Michelin stars, more than any other chef in the world. That's like winning the Tour de France ten times.

L'AVANT COMPTOIR DE L'ODÉON

9 Carrefour de l'Odéon - 75006 Paris
T +33 1 44 27 07 50

Daily 12.00-23.00

There are moments in L'Avant Comptoir – and recently also in its maritime sister, L'Avant Comptoir de la Mer – when I suspect there's an attempt to break the *Guinness Book of World Records* in the category of squeezing the maximum number of people into a very limited space.

You come and go as you please, order
wine if you feel like it, various tapas
when you're hungry

Small bites

L'Avant Comptoir is one of the trend-setters of the new breed of wine-bars-with-super-food, which is currently very popular in the French capital.

There are no places to sit here. There is a bar, a very nice wine list and a very impressive menu of tapas of impeccable quality prepared of course in the bar's kitchen.

While L'Avant Comptoir focuses on meat, L'Avant Comptoir de la Mer focuses completely on sea creatures in all their glory.

L'Avant Comptoir does not comply with the unwritten rules of eating and drinking; it doesn't take reservations, there are no chairs, and there are no special lunch and dinner offers. Total freedom reigns here: you come and go as you please, order wine if you feel like it, various tapas when you're hungry, and chat with the other guests around you. With a few platters of ham prepared by the legendary Eric Ospital and some good wine, total strangers become lifelong friends. This spot really counts as a social lubricant.

Yves Camdeborde, the owner and driving force of L'Avant Comptoir, is the French godfather of bistronomy to which he is totally devoted after his stints at The Ritz, Tour d'Argent and Crillon. He turned his back on luxury gastronomic temples and reinvented himself in his Comptoir du Relais restaurant, putting bistronomy in France on the map.

Both Avant Comptoirs are wonderful, informal spots that always make me forget about Wi-Fi and Whatsapp! If you're in Paris for only a day, this is the ideal spot to let the day pass by slowly and to observe life in Paris with a glass of Morgon.

RESTAURANT GUY SAVOY @ LA MONNAIE DE PARIS

11 Quai de Conti - 75006 Paris
T +33 1 43 80 40 61 - www.guysavoy.com
Tue–Fri: 12.00-14.00 and 19.00-22.30; Sat: 19.00-22.30

Two establishments in one. In 2015, Guy Savoy moved his 3-star restaurant to a very impressive location worthy of his name. He opted for a wing in the impressive building that housed the French *Monnaie de Paris* (Paris Mint Institute). Established in 864, this is the oldest French institute that still operates.

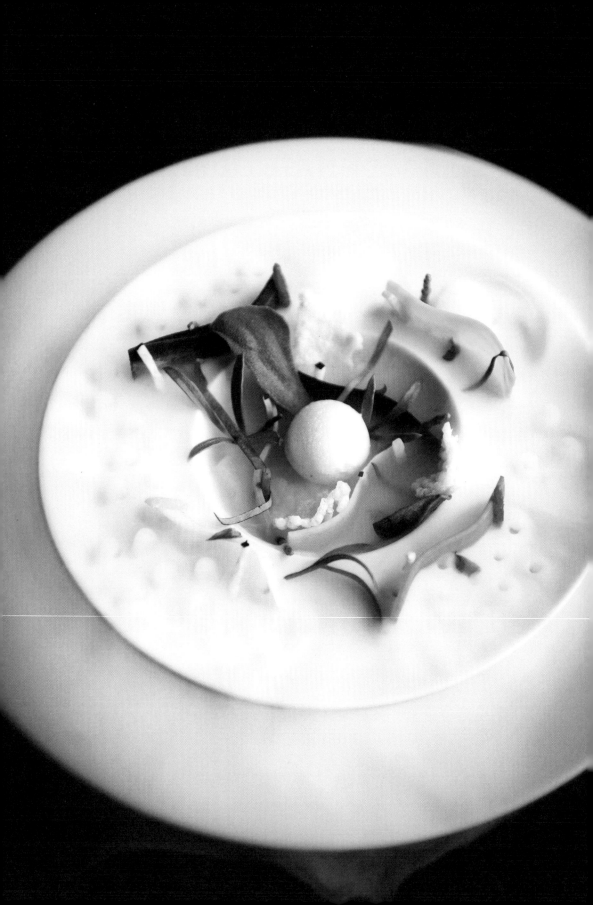

Menu innovations and inspirations in 12 sequences

In the Middle Ages, as a result of the partitioning into regions, there were naturally several locations where coins were manufactured, but the one in Paris still exists to a large degree as a benchmark unit.

The building is an example of the greatness of Paris and was designed by Jacques-Denis Antoine; its construction took no less than eight years, from 1767 to 1775. This first large project by Antoine is considered a climax of French Neoclassicism from pre-revolutionary France. The wide façade facing the Seine looks like a beautiful Italian palace.

If you look out the windows of this very impressive restaurant, you will see the banks of the Seine with lots of *bouquinistes*, the typical Parisian bookstalls. Down below people stroll romantically along the river or browse around the bookstalls. This relaxed atmosphere convinced Savoy to set up his restaurant at this location. No one wants to consume a magnificent meal with his favourite companions while people are rushing about in the restaurant. Guests want calmness around them so that they can relax. A breath of fresh air compared to the previous location that the restaurant occupied for 28 years on Rue Troyon in the 17th arrondissement.

Savoy is a living French monument. After completing his apprenticeship at Troisgros, he opened his own restaurant in New York City, but ultimately decided to return to Paris where he opened a restaurant in 1980 on Rue Duret. In five years he earned himself two Michelin stars. Gordon Ramsay considers Savoy his culinary mentor after completing several apprenticeships in his restaurant.

The restaurant consists of five impressive salons that interconnect. Even a giraffe can enter: the ceilings are practically endless. And yet the salons have an air of intimacy, literally a cocoon of warmth and safety. The entire place radiates obvious class. Large windows filter in light and ensure a unique atmosphere. A red neon display at the entrance reads: 'La cuisine est l'art de transformer en joie des produits chargés d'histoire' (Cooking is the art of transforming products steeped in history into instant joy) – an eccentric statement from someone knowledgeable. The kitchen brigade is especially happy with the new location. After working in a kitchen with only artificial light, this open kitchen offers daylight that penetrates through the beautiful window panes: the ideal environment to bring out the best in yourself.

Savoy does not idolize the past. On the contrary, he is more dynamic than ever and has a clear vision of the future. He has brought the famous Savoy taste into his new locations so that his loyal fans were also happy to move. Savoy has a cast-iron reputation which he lives up to by focusing on his work and his utmost respect for his products.

TOUR D'ARGENT

15 Quai de la Tournelle - 75005 Paris
T +33 1 43 54 23 31 - www.tourdargent.com
Tue.-Sat. open midday and evening

Tour d'Argent! An extraordinary name for an extraordinary restaurant. It was originally named L'Hostellerie de la Tour d'Argent by Rourteau, its founder and a famous chef in his time.

Tour d'Argent duck

This restaurant is one of the oldest restaurants in Europe which still operates and was established by Rourteau in 1582 – yes you read correctly. The restaurant was housed in a Renaissance tower covered with mica at the time. With the sun's rays on the mica, the tower had a completely silver shine. King Henry IV was a regular guest and was crazy about heron pâté and the renowned chicken in the pot.

At a certain point the restaurant and the place became so famous that Louis XIV, the Sun King himself, with his entire entourage travelled from Versailles to eat in the silver tower. Cardinal Richelieu was crazy about the goose with plums. He ordered an entire cow that had to be prepared in 30 different ways. This gallant feat went down in history and nowadays is still known as Beef Richelieu. This house of decadence flourished until 1789 when the French Revolution steamrollered it out of existence.

It was not until 1860 that this famous establishment emerged once again. When Karl Baedeker wrote that there is a small hotel with a well-kept and inexpensive restaurant between Notre-Dame and the Jardin des Plantes, Tour d'Argent came back into focus. In 1890, Frédéric Delair opened the restaurant and positioned it immediately on the gastronomic world map by creating the Tour d'Argent duck. This was a monumental dish and each guest that ate the restaurant's signature dish was presented a numbered certificate, a custom that continues to this day. And the ritual of placing the carcass of the duck in a pure silver press in order to obtain the basis for the sauce is still carried out, too. On 29 April 2003, the one millionth duck was served.

In 1918, the legendary André Terrail bought the entire establishment, and after World War I he handed over the kitchen to François Lespinas. The restaurant quickly regained its glorious position, a place where celebrities from all over the world came to dine. Regular guests of the restaurant included Marcel Proust and Salvador Dalí. While André was building the world famous George V Hotel in 1936, he took the opportunity to renovate the Tour d'Argent, giving it the look that's almost the same today. The famous Michelin restaurant guide had given it three stars, already back in 1933. Claude Terrail, André's son, managed the silver tower through a number of turbulent years and nowadays leaves the daily operations to his son, André.

The kitchen is run by Philippe Labbé, who has the difficult task of ensuring that Tour d'Argent remains a culinary place of pilgrimage with classics such as brouillades aux truffes (scrambled eggs with truffles), quenelles de brochet diaphanes (delicate pike quenelles), caneton mazarine à l'orange (duckling in orange sauce), Princess Elisabeth soufflé and of course the Tour d'Argent duck.

The motto of the house is 'nothing is worse than pleasure' and they have certainly succeeded in realising this with their cellar of 400,000 bottles of fine wines.

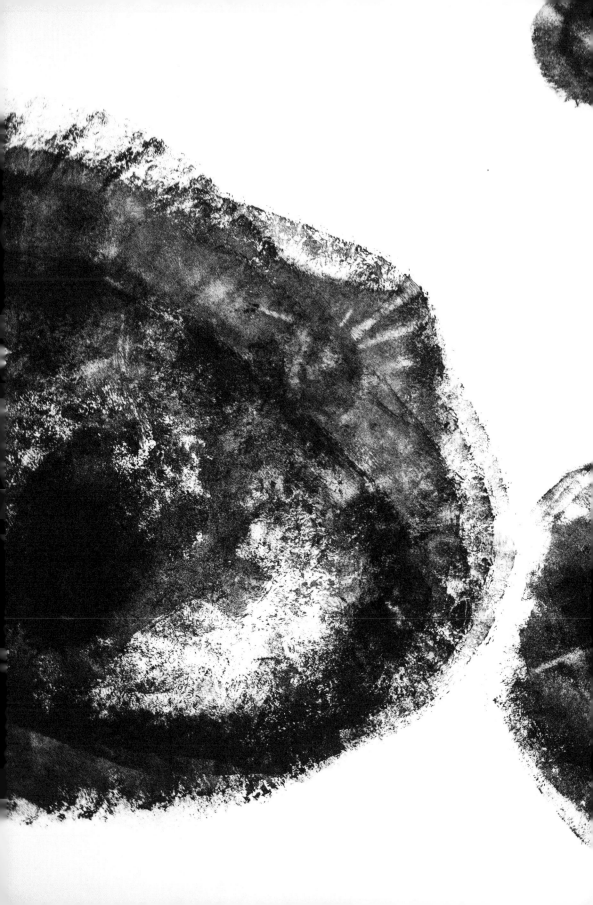

ADDITIONAL EATERIES
SAINT-GERMAIN-DES-PRÉS / MONTPARNASSE / JARDIN DES PLANTES

CHINATOWN OLYMPIADES
44 Avenue D'Ivry, 75013 Paris
T +33 1 45 84 72 21
www.chinatownolympiades.com
Mon.-Sun. 11.45-14.45 and 18.45-01.00

GODJO
8 Rue de l'École Polytechnique, 75005 Paris
T +33 1 40 46 82 21
www.godjo.com
Mon.-Sun. 12.00-02.00

L'AUBERGE DU 15
15 Rue de la Santé, 75013 Paris
T +33 1 47 07 07 45
www.laubergedu15.com
Thu.-Sat. 12.00-14.00 and 19.00-23.00

LE DRAPEAU DE LA FIDÉLITÉ
21 Rue Copreaux, 75015 Paris
T +33 1 45 66 73 82
Mon.-Sun. 11.30-22.00

LES PAPILLES
30 Rue Gay-Lussac, 75005 Paris
T +33 1 43 25 20 79
www.lespapillesparis.fr
Thu.-Sat. 12.00-14.00 and 19.00-22.30

LI KA FO
39 Avenue de Choisy, 75013 Paris
T +33 1 45 84 20 45
Mon.-Sun. 12.00-23.00

RELAIS DE LOUIS XIII
8 Rue des Grands Augustins, 75006 Paris
T +33 1 43 26 75 96
www.relaislouis13.fr
Thu.-Sat. 12.15-14.30 and 19.30-22.30

ZE KITCHEN GALLERY
4 Rue des Grands Augustins, 75006 Paris
T +33 1 44 32 00 32
www.zekitchengalerie.fr
Mon.-Fri. 12.00-14.30 and 19.30-23.00

ARPÈGE

84 Rue de Varenne - 75007 Paris
T +33 1 47 05 09 06 - www.alain-passard.com
Mon.-Fri. 12.00-14.30 and 19.00-22.30

If we now had to pick the most influential, eccentric and modest chef in Paris, it would no doubt be the visionary trendsetter, Alain Passard. It is impossible to imagine today's haute gastronomy without him.

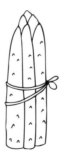

He has trained many chefs who are now considered the absolute best. He has taught Pascal Barbot and David Toutain the tricks of the trade of a top chef.

Dining at Arpège is a rare privilege, a moment to cherish, like a first kiss. Passard hails from Brittany where his parents were professionally occupied with music, a totally different form of art. Alain is still quite good with a saxophone.

He himself considers David Kinch, the celebrated chef of the Californian Restaurant, Manresa, as his absolute example and his greatest inspiration. Passard worked for a while with Alain Senderens in L'Archestrate, a restaurant at the corner of Rue de Varenne and Rue de Bourgogne. In 1986, he bought the place from Senderens and rechristened it Arpège, as tribute to his love for music.

In 2001, he began his quest for the ideal vegetables. His menus are based on seasonal products and he tries to buy only naturally and organically grown products from hobby growers and artisanal farmers. He conceived an ingenious system for producing ideal vegetables. He planted three vegetable gardens in three totally different micro climates. The first was in Sarthe, the second in Eure and the third in Manche. Three gardens in three different areas of origin give the vegetables their specific soil signature: the sand in Sarthe for carrots, asparagus and leek, the clay of Eure for celery and cabbages and the alluvial soil in Manche for aromatic herbs. Twelve gardeners work with donkeys, cows, hens and goats in this ambitious and successful project that – as you might have noticed yourself – has gained quite a following in international haute gastronomy. These vegetable plots produce around 40 tons and that makes Passard the only restaurateur who is fully self-sufficient when it comes to vegetables, herbs and red & black fruit. Each morning, the harvest from the three gardens is transported to Paris. The fruit and vegetables never see the inside of a refrigerator.

There is something about visionary geniuses that sets them apart, because 99.99% of the world does not agree with their ideas, no matter what. It took thirty years for Passard to be convinced that he had become a *maître rôtisseur* (king of the grill) and to be praised internationally for

Vintage vegetables

his subtle and exquisite cooking of meat, only to remove meat from his menu in 2001, because it no longer inspired him. For Passard, the vegetable-oriented cuisine contains so many surprises, because so far so little had been done with a tomato or an eggplant, for example. His fruit and vegetables are genuinely *grand cru* (vintage) and require minimal intervention in the kitchen. And since molecular cuisine now reigns the restaurant scene, his philosophy is less popular these days.

I would never buy a recipe book by Passard, because you never start out with the same raw materials. What I would rather buy is a book about Passard's philosophy. (Hey, that's something to discuss one day with my publisher!) If someone truly respects the seasons, everything will happen automatically. What grows together should also be served together on a plate. Striking but astounding are the fruit and vegetable combination: peach with red pepper, cucumber with strawberry, courgette and fig, tomato with pear.

A few meals ago, I was greatly impressed by a simple bowl with fresh garden peas, fresh mint and pink grapefruit. These combinations sometimes seem unreal until you taste them.

I am totally convinced that Passard's decision to endow vegetables with a main role in his restaurant was a very significant moment in culinary history. He started a major trend and – as always – all the rest have tried to proclaim that they reinvented the wheel. But let us get one fact straight: Arpège is by no means a vegetarian restaurant. Although the vegetable gardens constitute the foundation of his kitchen, they are definitely not the alpha and omega of what is happening here. Arpège also serves turbot, duck, top-quality fowl and much more. This kitchen is busy with far more than letting the ingredients speak for themselves. Passard's cooking style not only isolates and captures the essence of the ingredients, but transforms them into dishes with results that are greater than the sum of their parts. His minimalism is more like optimization.

His kitchen is his interpretation of the season and offers a rare look at how a season should really taste. The one and only real maestro. What are you waiting for?

CHEZ DUMONET

117 Rue du Cherche-Midi - 75006 Paris
T +33 1 45 48 52 40
Mon.-Fri. 12.00-14.30 and 19.30-21.30

Chez Dumonet, or Joséphine as many people call this restaurant, is an irresistible
Parisian bistro where time stands still.

Bœuf bourguignon

French country cuisine that Escoffier has elevated
into the greatest culinary art

The only compromise made to modern times is that certain dishes can also be ordered in half portions, although even these can be too heavy on the stomach. The kitchen of Jean-Christian Dumonet is rich and tasty. You can recognise the regular guests by the fact that they are a few sizes bigger than the waiters.

You come here to experience Paris of pre-WW1, as if through a sepia filter. It is a lovely art-nouveau bistro on a fancy street in Saint-Germain. It looks as if nothing has changed since 1880, the year that the building was built and when it was still a *bougnat*, a local café that also sold coal. This is an unmistakable place to go to if you want to enjoy old-school dishes, a place where the 35-hour workweek still doesn't determine which labour-intensive dishes will be on the menu. One of the highlights is the bœuf bourguignon, a typical dish from Bourgogne in which beef and minced veal are cooked long and slow in red wine. In other words, French country cuisine that Escoffier has elevated into the greatest culinary art.

This is a genuine spot-on Parisian bistro, the type threatened by extinction. Close your eyes, picture a beautiful French movie, and imagine a scene where the protagonists are eating in a restaurant. You'll find it difficult to find a better tribute to the classic Parisian bistro.

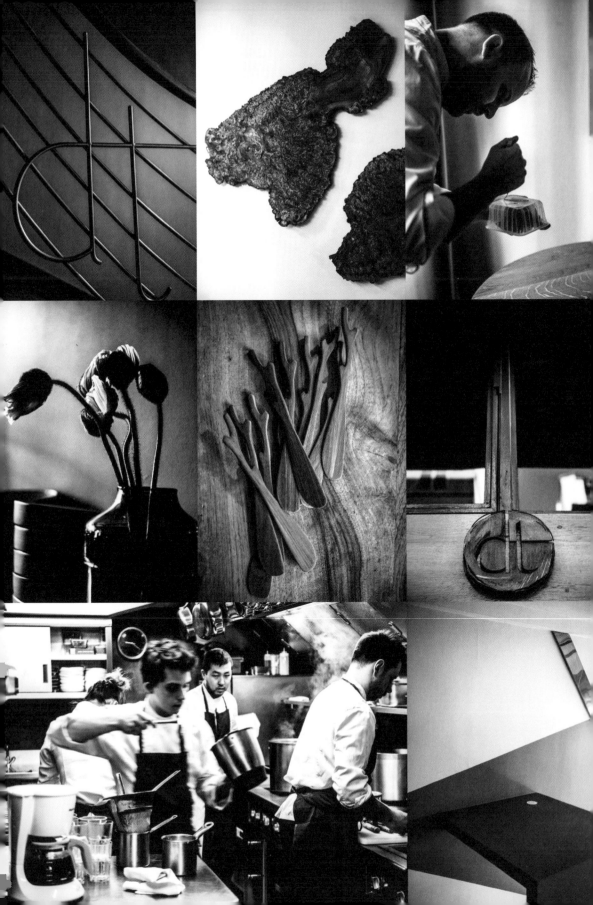

DAVID TOUTAIN

29 Rue Surcouf - 75007 Paris
T +33 1 45 50 11 10 - www.davidtoutain.com
Mon.-Fri. 12.00-14.30 and 20.00-22.00

Chefs have a lot to say, but regrettably, many don't express themselves via their skills and dishes. They prefer to use other channels for that and they are often more occupied with building their image. That's too bad, because gastronomy lends itself to expressing points of view and emotions.

DAVID TOUTAIN

Egg

Rarely have I met a more modest and honest chef than Toutain, who evokes the mysticism of the *kabuki* theatre. This is a fellow who knows what he wants, knows what he is capable of and above all, knows what he cannot do. The latter is a typical characteristic of people who go far in the world. When he was twenty, he began working for Alain Passard who, at the time, was perfecting his vegetable dishes. One year later, he became Passard's right-hand man. Afterwards he moved to Gagnaire and subsequently to Pacaud and Veyrat. Mugaritz and Tribal (New York City) were also stops along the way.

Before he stood on his own two feet, he worked at Agapè Substance where he wiped away any doubts about his exceptional talent. Restaurant David Toutain is a fact and, as far as I'm concerned, it goes down in the annals of a success story.

A meal at Toutain is served in Omakase style in which ten dishes prepared in the kitchen make it crystal-clear that its culinary ambitions are of the highest. This austere restaurant emanates an almost ascetic atmosphere with a high sense of Zen. The ascetic character can also be seen in the monumental simplicity of the dishes, put together with a strong sense for composition. The exceptional sense for basic products, which runs like a leitmotiv through Toutain's work of art and that most likely already began at Passsard, is exemplary.

Just like Mick Jagger's assertion that after several thousands of concerts he still gets a little stage fright, Toutain's greatest concern is that his guest are presented with a perfect dish – every time. Toutain is nothing less than the culinary incarnation of what is known in the art world as a masterpiece. Do yourself a favour and come and dine here as soon as possible. This is the type of restaurant that creates great memories.

L'AMI JEAN

27 Rue Malar - 75007 Paris
T +33 1 47 05 86 89 - www.lamijean.fr
Tue.-Sat. 12.00-14.30 and 19.00-00.00

In 2002, Stéphane Jégo and his wife Sandrine took over the Basque establishment, l'Ami Jean, after Stéphane had worked there for twelve years with another pioneer of French bistronomy, Yves Camdeborde.

L'Ami Jean experience

Together they were the kitchen talents behind the legendary La Régalade. L'Ami Jean is located in a quiet street close to the Eiffel Tower and it is a noisy, enormously busy bistro, and probably one of the most popular in Paris. When it opened in 1931, it was influenced by Basque nationalism, but the choice of food of a super talent such as Jégo goes way beyond the Basque region.

L'Ami Jean is difficult to classify and I have absolutely no problem with this. It fits simultaneously into various categories, which is why the clientele is so diversified. The average guest has a strong affection for rock-'n-roll and visitors should not be alarmed by the size of the portions. The walls are painted with cartoons and large pieces of ham hang from the ceiling next to crystals chandeliers.

I'm always happy to describe the l'Ami Jean experience: Jégo, whose loud voice bellows out of the kitchen, ordering his waiters to hurry up, the well-managed chaos and of course the insanely good food makes dining here a special experience. Your first l'Ami Jean trip is either heavenly or you don't know what you're talking about.

Jégo's kitchen is shamelessly brilliant. This man has an absolute new definition of comfort food and generosity. Although he uses only with the best seasonal products – which he posts daily on social media – his favourite season is the autumn. Sending half-eaten plates back to the kitchen is not tolerated and when you're done making your excuses, the waiters serve you a giant portion of rice pudding to fill in the holes.

Indeed, Jégo's kitchen style cannot be pigeonholed. Gastronomy? Bistronomy? His kitchen is defined by sharing flavours, sharing the joy of life, emotions and moments. His kitchen emanates generosity and bravado. Jégo is happy to share his passion and love for his trade with his guests, who literally fight to get a reservation. And from the dining area it is always a pleasure to see the chef busy in his kitchen.

It is a great restaurant where you eat as if it's your last meal. I recommend a stroll back home or to your hotel to walk off a few pounds. When you're standing on the scales the next morning, you will be grateful for this tip.

Stéphane Jégo for President!

SYLVESTRE

79 Rue Saint-Dominique - 75007 Paris
T +33 1 47 05 79 00 - www.thoumieux.fr
Thu-Fri. 12.30-14.30; Tue., Wed. & Sat. 19.30-22.00

For a long time, the Thoumieux was under the wings of
top-notch chef, Jean-François Piège.

WAHID!

Inspiration of the day

When the latter decided to leave in order to start his own restaurant in the 8th arrondissement, Thierry Costes wasted no time and began to search for a worthy successor. He didn't need a Ronaldo or a Messi for this place; he resolutely opted for a wise and methodical chef.

Sylvestre Wahid, who has a very impressive track record, was born 40 years ago in Kohat, Pakistan, where he was called Shahzad. At the age of nine, he fled Pakistan with his mother and came to France, arriving in Roissy. They settled and integrated in Nîmes. Shahzad became Sylvestre and he fell in love with his new fatherland. It was love at first sight when, at the age of 16, he discovered truffles, skewered suckling pig and Pommard wine. An apprenticeship at a fancy bakery con-firmed his enthusiasm and he decided to study at a hotel school. Thierry Marx was very impressed by him during the apprenticeship. In Plaza Athénée he was noticed by Ducasse and ironically he worked at that time in Ducasse's kitchen under chef Jean-François Piège.

Sylvestre's kitchen reflects his personality: calm and focused. The dining room, renovated by India Mahdavi, enhances his pastoral kitchen, which is tranquil, yet technically complex. This kitchen is naturally exalting and full of refined details. This catches on in the City of Lights, although succeeding a chef such as Piège is no easy task; after all, you are always compared to him. A wonderful, sensitive and talented man in splendid interior decor… it doesn't get much better.

TAN DINH

60 Rue de Verneuil - 75007 Paris
T +33 1 45 44 04 84
Mon.-Sat. 12.00-14.00 and 19.30-23.00

Freddy and Robert Vifian are both concepts in the world of Parisian restaurants and beyond. Their restaurant has become a real cult in Paris. One of the best wine lists is combined here with traditional Vietnamese food with a modern twist.

Smoked goose ravioli

Robert came to Paris with his grandmother in 1968 after the fall of Saigon to join his parents who were already living there. With four hungry mouths to feed, his parents decided to open a restaurant. That resulted in Tan Dinh, which the brothers have run for the last thirty years.

This is no doubt the oldest Vietnamese restaurant in the city. Tan Dinh does not follow fashion, trends or stars; it's the type of restaurant that follows its own path and which people discover almost by accident.

Robert, who was born in Saigon in 1948, is an autodidact and one of the most enigmatic personalities in the gastronomic microcosmos, also known as Paris. His passion for great wines – he scribbles down all his comments in his notebook – is coupled with his passion for modern art, more specifically Basquiat, Haring and his good friend, Canadian sculptor, David Altmejd.

In his restaurant he feels at home, safe like a sea urchin in its prickly shell. The Vietnamese kitchen does have its own unique identity, although it

is evolving into the fast food culture where that identity regretfully gets lost or transformed into Pho, a national dish of Vietnam. Tan Dinh, which means new city, naturally doesn't go along with this and it should not be overlooked if you want to discover the Vietnamese kitchen in all its tradition and splendour.

If there is one restaurant in the world which I feel I should visit more often, it is Tan Dinh. Not only for the delicious food and phenomenal wine list, but also for the human side of the Vifian brothers which makes it so much more than just a restaurant. Robert became an international wine icon and takes pride in his encyclopaedic knowledge. He enjoys immense respect from wine experts such as Robert Parker, Michel Bettane and Steven Spurrier. His quest began after reading Curnonsky, who said: "When the Asiatic kitchen is perfectly marinated with wine, it undoubtedly becomes the best in the world."

Professionals beyond doubt with a noble disposition, such people must be cherished and occupy a place in your heart, never to be forgotten.

ADDITIONAL EATERIES

TOUR EIFFEL /
LES INVALIDES /
MUSÉE D'ORSAY

AIDA
1 Rue Pierre Leroux, 75007 Paris
T +33 1 43 06 14 18
www.aida-paris.net
Tue.-Sun. 19.30-21.00